NATURE & LIFE IN POEMS

--- PARTS I & II ---

DR. BELLARIO AHOY NGONG GENG

The ideas and opinions in this book are ultimately those of the author. Their authenticity is the responsibility of the author, not Africa World Books.

The publisher wishes to acknowledge and thank Dr Douglas H. Johnson for his invaluable help and support for Africa World Books and its mission of preserving and promoting African cultural and literary traditions and history. Dr Johnson and fellow historians have been instrumental in ensuring that African people remain connected to their past and their identity. Africa World Books is proud to carry on this mission.

© Dr. Bellario Ahoy Ngong Geng, 2022, All rights reserved.

ISBN: 978-0-6454529-3-8

No part of this publication may be reproduced, stored in a retrieval system, or transmitted, in any form, or by any means, electronic, mechanical, photocopying, recording or otherwise, without the prior permission of the publishers.

This book is sold subject to the conditions that it shall not, by way of trade or otherwise, be lent, re-sold, hired out or otherwise circulated without the publisher's prior consent in any form of binding or cover other than in which it is published and without a similar condition including the condition being imposed on the subsequent purchaser.

Cover design, typesetting and layout : Africa World Books

DEDICATION

In memory of my dear parents;
Ngong Geng Mathiang, my father
& Kuei Tiop Kut, my mother.
Both were traditional poets.

CONTENTS

ACKNOWLEDGMENT	XXVII
PREFACE	XXIX
INTRODUCTION	XXI
CHAPTER I: ABOUT MY SELF AND LOCALITY	1
AWEIL	1
THE YEAR OF MY BIRTH (1951)	2
LOCATION SPOT OF MY BIRTH	2
MY FIRST SCHOOL (1959)	3
MY FIRST TEACHER (I)	3
MY FIRST TEACHER (II)	4
MY INTERMEDIATE SCHOOL (1963-1964)	5
SUNDAY STRIKE OF 1964	5
MY SECONDARY SCHOOL (1969)	6
MY MEDICAL STUDIES IN ALEXANDERIA (1973)	6
WORKING AS AN INTERN (1980)	7
POSTED TO WAU HOSPITAL (1981)	8
TWO YEARS AT GOGRIAL HOSPITAL (1981-83)	8
TWO YEARS AT AWEIL HOSPITAL (1983-85)	9
POST GRADUATE IN KHARTOUM (1986-88)	9
WITH CARE INTERNATIONAL AT NAHUD (1988)	10

AT THE MINISTRY OF HEALTH IN KHARTOUM (1989)	11
MALARIA COURSE IN THAILAND AND ITALY (1990)	11
JOINING SPLM IN 1990	12
MILITARY TRAINING IN 1991	12
POSTED TO KAPOETA (1991)	13
COMMISSIONED CAPTAIN IN 1992	13
SURGEON IN ASHWA HOSPITAL (1992)	14
POSTED TO MUNDRI (1992)	15
POSTED TO AKON IN 1993	15
AS HEALTH COORDINATOR FOR NORTHERN BHAR-EL-GHAZAL (1994)	16
HEALTH COORDINATOR FOR SPLM AREAS (1998)	16
A DELEGATE TO CPA TALKS (2003)	17
AS COMMISSIONER OF SRRC (2005)	17
CHAIRPERSON OF HIV/AIDS COMMISSION (2006)	18
GENTLEMAN OF TIARALIET (I)	19
GENTLEMAN OF TIARALIET (II)	19
GENTLEMAN OF TIARALIET (III)	20
LADY OF TIARALIET	20
MILE 14 (KIIR ADEM)	21

PART I

CHAPTER II: RELATIONS AND BEHAVIOUR	23
HOW EASILY YOU CAN FORGET	23
KINGDOM OF UNGRATEFULNESS	24
TAKEN FOR A RIDE	24
CORRUPTION (I)	25
CORRUPTION (II) (NECK AND HEAD DISEASE)	26
CORRUPTION ON DEFENSIVE	27
CORRUPT PERSONALITY VERSUS FAIR PERSONALITY	28
EVERYWHERE SURROUNDED BY CORRUPTION (I)	29
EVERYWHERE SURROUNDED BY CORRUPTION (II)	30

I'M INNOCENT	31
TEMPLE OF MY KINDNESS	32
TREE TOP	32
THE HARDWORK REWARD	33
WEALTH (I)	33
WEALTH (II)	34
WEALTH (III)	34
WEALTH (IV)	35
JUSTICE	35
THE JOY OF RECEIVING	36
LOVE	37
LOVERS	37
GIVE THEM A PROPER NAME(I)	38
GIVE THEM A PROPER NAME (II)	38
GIVE THEM THE PROPER NAME (III)	39
FATE OF HUMAN VALUES (JUSTICE, FAIRNESS, EQUALITY, TRANSPARENCY, HONESTY)	39
SELFISHNESS	40
HIDDEN HATRED	41
THERE IS ALWAYS A DOOR TO OPEN	41
HOPE	42
LUCK	42
FRIEND	43
NEIGHBOR	43
MOTHER	44
FATHER	45
SON	45
DAUGHTER	46
SISTER	46
BROTHER	47
IF I HAVE A BROTHER	47
YET YOU CALL ME A BROTHER	48

UNCLE	49
AUNT	49
NIECE	50
NEPHEW	50
GRAND FATHER	51
GRAND MOTHER	52
GRAND SON	52
GRAND DAUGHTER	53
DYNAMICS OF RICHES	53
THIS IS A QUEER WORLD	54
HIDING REAL INTENTIONS	55
THE AGONY OF LONELINESS	56
GRATEFULNESS	56
UNGRATEFULNESS (I)	57
UNGRATEFULNESS (II)	58
HOW TO GET WHAT YOU WANT	58
COWARDICE AND BRAVERY	59
LIAR AND TRUTH TELLER	60
GOOD AND BAD PERSON	60
GOOD AND BAD PERSON	61
FRIENDSHIP	61
ESCAPE FROM LEOPARD CLAWS	62
HATRED	63
DIALOGUE BETWEEN WELL TO DO AND LESS TO DO	63
INSPECTORS' TIP	64
FROM FRYING PAN TO FIRE	64
ON BEING A MAVERICK	65
THE WHEEL OF JUSTICE TURNS SLOW	66
RUMOUR IS TALL AND RUNS FASTER	66
TRUTH IS SMALL, THIN AND HANDSOME	67
A LIE IS TALL, FAST AND UGLY	67
WHEN TIME TICKS TOO SLOW	68

WHEN TIME IS TICKING TOO FAST	69
CRITICISM	69
HOME IS HOME	70
MY PEOPLE	70
REACTIONS OF PEOPLE TO INSULTS	71
MORAL NATURE OF PEOPLE	72
PARADOXES OF LIFE (I)	72
PARADOXES OF LIFE (II)	73
PARADOXES OF LIFE (III)	73
PARADOXES OF LIFE (IV)	74
PEOPLE AND WHAT THEY DO	75
RESOURCES AND PEOPLE'S RELATIONS	75
PANACEA TO ALL WORLD'S PROBLEMS (A REMINDER)	76
IN PEACE WITH MYSELF	76
IN PEACE WITH OTHERS	77
BRIDE	77
BRIDE GROOM	78
THE YOUNG GENERATION (I)	79
THE YOUNG GENERATION (II)	79
HUMAN BEHAVIOR AND WEALTH	80
HUMAN BEHAVIOR ANALYSED (I)	81
HUMAN BEHAVIOR ANALYSED (II)	82
HUMAN BEHAVIOR ANALYSED (III)	83
WOLVES IN SHEEP CLOTHES	84
RELATIONS ARE FUNCTION OF INTERESTS	86
IF THIEVES ARE GETTING FAT THE VICTIMS MUST BE GETTING THIN	87
IMPORTANCE OF EDUCATION (I)	88
IMPORTANCE OF EDUCATION (II)	88
NO THEY ARE NOT MAD THEY ARE FOOLS	89
PASSING THROUGH A HOLE OF A NEEDLE (I) (A DIALOGUE BETWEEN YOUNG PEOPLE AND AN ELDER)	91

PASSING THROUGH A HOLE OF A NEEDLE (II)	
(A DIALOGUE BETWEEN YOUNG PEOPLE AND AN ELDER)	92
PRIVATE INTEREST VERSUS PUBLIC INTEREST	93
SELFISHNESS IS THE ROOT CAUSE OF ALL WOES	94
THE SOURCE OF A FATAL BLOW	94
WHEN YOUR CALLS ARE RECEIVED WITH JOY	95
WHEN YOUR CALLS ARE RECEIVED WITH	96
RELUCTANCE	97
OLD AND YOUNG PERSONS	97
EFFECT OF BLIND SUPPORT	98
I KNOW YOU	99
WHO IS A GOOD FRIEND?	100
WHO IS A FAKE FRIEND?	100
FINDING A GOOD WIFE OR HUSBAND TO BE	101
MY AGE MATES	102
THE DAY I FELT LONELY	102
VALUE OF A DIALOGUE	103
OBITUARY POEM	104
NATURE WHY TAKE AWAY MY BROTHER?	104
RECEPTION OF TRAGEDY AT TIARLAIET	105
WITH HUMAN NATURE ANY TREATMENT YOU WILL GET	105
BRIDE THROWN OUT OF WINDOW	106
ROOTS OF A PERSON	107
THE DISTRESS CAUSED BY RECKLESS CHILDREN	108
MARITAL RELATIONS	108
TREASON	109
WHEN FORMER ENEMIES BECOME FRIENDS	110
PUBLIC SERVICE VERSUS PRIVATE SERVICE	111
DEEP IN DEBT	111
PRAYERS OF THE DECEIVED AND HUMILIATED	112
WHEN TWO MIGHTY FIGHT	113
TIME TO HARVEST	113

CHAPTER III: NATURE AND ITS FEATURES	115
NATURE OF MEN	115
NATURE OF WOMEN	116
DO NOT DISTURB MOTHER NATURE	116
THE RAPE OF JEBEL KUJUR	117
NATURE OF PROBLEMS	118
IN ACCORD WITH NATURE	118
NATURE OF LIFE	119
RIVER	119
RAIN	120
I ENVY WATER AND AIR	121
IMPORTANCE OF WATER	121
WATER NEVER DIES	122
I'M CALLED WATER	122
CONQUERER OF INJUSTICE (I)	123
CONQUERER OF INJUSTICE (II)	124
DOG	124
COW	125
FOREST	126
SUN	126
AT THE MERCY OF THE SUN	127
THE SUNSET HAZE	127
MOON	128
WIND	129
AIR	129
WATER MELON	130
CHICKEN	130
HEN AND EGG MYSTERY	131
THE MORNING BREEZE	132
THE STILL NIGHT	133
USEFUL INSECTS (BEES)	133
BEES	134

BEES ON THE OFFENSIVE	134
MAHOGANY	135
TAMARIND TREE	136
BENEFITS OF LALOOB TREE	136
EBONY	137
MALARIA	137
MOSQUITO	138
INTESTINAL WORMS	139
FISH	139
TALAPIA FISH	140
A DIALOGUE WITH A SNAKE	140
WHEN EARTH BECOMES HELL	142
WHEN EARTH BECOMES HEAVEN	142
THE VALUE OF HOPE	143
DEATH	143
THE VALUE OF DEATH	144
FIRE	145
DIALOGUE WITH FIRE	145
DESERT	146
SCORPION	147
SCORPION AND FROG IN A JOKE GAME	148
EVIDENCE OF AN HEALTH ENVIRONMENT	148
HEALTH	149
LIFE IS WALKING ON A TIGHT ROPE	149
VISIBLE AND INVISIBLE	150
ESSENCE OF LIFE	151
GOOD AND BAD	151
CHAPTER IV: POWER AND INSTITUTIONS OF POLITICS	153
CONSTITUTION	153
MY COUNTRY	154
PARLIAMENT	154

EXECUTIVE	155
ANGEL AND DEVIL WORLDS	155
EFFECT OF HIGH LEVEL DECISIONS	156
POWER AND RIGHT	157
WHEN ALCOHOL, LUST AND MONEY ARE SERVANTS OF KING LION	157
FATE OF POLITICAL GROUPINGS	159
YOU ARE STRANGE MY COUNTRY	159
POLITICAL JUSTICE DILEMMA	160
LEGACY OF A DEAD LEADER	161
DEMOCRACY	161
THE FALSE LIBERATOR	162
DEMOCRACY THE ULTIMATE GOAL	163
GOOD AND BAD LEADER	164
PREROGATIVE OF A SOVEREIGN	165
A LEADER	165
FATE OF A DESPOTIC SOVEREIGN	166
COST AND BENEFITS OF LIBERATION	166
THE DEMISE OF THE LIBERATORS	167
FREEDOM WHERE ARE YOU?	167
DIALOGUE BETWEEN MR. INQUISITIVE AND MR. FREEDOM FIGHTER	168
POLITICIANS	169
DESPOT HAS NO COLOR (A DIALOGUE BETWEEN MR. INQUISITIVE AND MR. WISE)	170
POLITICS (BLIND, DEAF AND SELFISH)	171
POWER SO SWEET	171
OFFICE OF POLITICS	172
RIGHTS ARE FOR A STRONG	173
SOLUTION OF A COUNTRY PROBLEMS BY DIVISION	173
REVOLUTIONS AND THEIR FATE	174
WORRY ABOUT THE BABY (NATION)	175

REINSTATEMENT OF A TYRANT	175
A STRAIGHT STICK IS CROOKED IN WATER	176
EXHORTATION FOR NATIONAL UNITY	176
WHETHER POLITICS ARE GOOD OR BAD	177
COUNTRY AND RULERS	178
ADVICE TO EARS THAT CAN HEAR	178
POWER CYCLE IN A GIVEN SYSTEM	179
PEOPLE, LEADERS AND POWER	180
POWER IS A POLITICAL ALCOHOL	180
TO BE A NATIONAL HERO	181
THE FAVORITES OF A LEADER	181
ABSOLUTE POWER	182
POWER DYNAMICS	183
LEADER, PEOPLE AND TRUST	183
RUNNING OUT OF A REVOLUTIONARY STEAM	184
HOW TO GAIN POWER	185
FREEDOM ELABORATED	186
ARDENT FREEDOM SUPPORTER	186
DIVISION IS A FUNCTION OF INTEREST, IT HAS NO END	188
TASTES OF POWER	188
THE KING MAKER	190
ON DEFENSE OF POLITICAL NAIVETY	190
LEADERS THAT BARK AND HOWL WITHOUT ACTION	191
FREEDOM IN FOCUS (I)	192
FREEDOM IN FOCUS (II)	193
PRAYERS OF SELFISH LEADERS	194
LIBERATION GOAL PATH	194
THE RULE OF FORCE	195
PEACE AND WAR	196
GOING ON AN ERRAND	196
WHEN TWO ELEPHANTS FIGHT	197
POWER IS A FACTOR	198

THE NECESSITY OF A LEADERSHIP CHANGE	199
HOW LEADERS LOSE	199
LEADERSHIP RIVALRY	200
LIVING WITH POWER GIANTS	201
A WARLORD	201
I STOOD IN AWE	202
SELFISHNESS IS STRONGER THAN NATIONALISM	202
QUEER ARE HUMAN BEINGS!	203
HOW CLEVER THEY ARE	204
WHAT POWER IS LIKE	204
EDUCATED PERSON DISEASE	205
UNEDUCATED PERSON DISEASE	206
PLEA OF ONCE A TYRANT	206
RESPONSE OF PEOPLE TO A TYRANT PLEA	207
BEHAVIOR OF A WEAK PERSONALITY	208
LOST IN THE FOREST (WHAT CAN WE DO?)	209
SENIOR HUNTER ADVICE TO YOUNG HUNTER	209
SENSATION AND POWER	210
COLD WAR (DEFINED)	211
COLD WAR TACTICS (DIVIDE AND RULE)	211
COLD WAR TACTICS (ECONOMIC SANCTION)	212
COLD WAR TACTICS (JOB DENIAL)	212
COLD WAR TACTICS (SCAPEGOAT)	213
COLD WAR TACTICS (HYPOCRISY)	214
COLD WAR TACTICS (SABOTAGE)	214
CHILDREN OF MY COUNTRY	215
LEADERS AND THEIR SERVICES	216
IF YOU WANT TO BE	216
PEACE AND WAR	217
PEOPLE, LEADERS AND WEALTH	218
TWO WAYS OF GAINING POWER	218

CHAPTER V: MISCELLANEOUS	219
INJUSTICE NEVER DIES	219
JUDICIARY	230
LOOKING FOR MY RIGHT	220
EVERY NATION HAS A HEAD, BODY AND TAIL	221
MOUNTAIN ON MY ROAD	221
PRISON	222
REAL FREEDOM	223
AT LAST CROCODILE IS MADE A CHIEF	223
HOW WOLF BECAME A SHEPHERD	224
SELF IMPOSED VIGILANTE	225
THE BEST WE HAVE	226
THIEVES IN A SYSTEM	227
MEAT AND HUNGRY DOGS	228
FIGHTING WITH A LION	229
INSECTS PICKED THE GAUNTLET	229
GUEST HAS GROWN HORNS	230
PATRIOTISM	231
HIGH POPULARITY (I)	231
HIGH POPULARITY (II)	232
EQUALITY BEFORE LAW	233
COURTS AND THEIR LIMITS (I)	235
COURTS AND THEIR LIMITS (II)	235
IF SUSPECTED THIEVES QUARREL THE REAL THIEF WILL BE FOUND	236
JUDGES ARE ALSO HUMAN	237
ESCAPING TOWARDS EAST	238
PANTHOU	239
WHY ARE THEY HARSH ON ME ALONE	240
HE CAME BACK AGAIN AND GAVE A FATAL BELOW	240
CHILD IS WEANED FOR ANOTHER TO COME	241
CHILD ONCE BORN CAN NOT BE RETURNED TO A WOMB	241

INFORMATION	242
REPENT AND WILL BE FORGIVEN	243
KINDS OF PRISONS	243
KNOWLEDGE	244

PART II
CHAPTER II: RELATIONS AND BEHAVIOUR — 245

THE ASSASSINS OF LION KING	245
THERE IS A RARE CHANCE TO SLAP A KING	246
RICH AND POOR	246
A DIALOGUE WITH A SELFISH GREEDY PERSON	247
A LIAR WHO SAVED A MAN'S LIFE	248
EFFECT OF HATRED	249
WHEN RIGHTS MIX UP WITH WRONG	249
PEOPLE OF LIMITED ASSISTANCE	250
BEWARE OF HYPOCRITES	251
EVERYONE HAS A HUMAN OBSTACLE/PROMOTER IN LIFE	251
LANDS LODGE COMPLAINTS	252
BEHAVIOR OF RICHES	252
RIGHTEOUS PATH VERSUS CROOKED PATH (I)	253
RIGHTEOUS PATH VERSUS CROOKED PATH (II)	254
BANKING DILEMMA (I)	255
BANKING DILEMMA (II)	256
JOBLESS	257
BEHIND THE SMILING FACES	257
WALKING PROUDLY	258
CATCHING A THIEF	259
ESSENCE OF GOOD RELATIONS	259
WHAT IS AT STAKE	260
NO PLACE FOR TENDER HEART IN THE WORLD	261
TIME CAN BE A SOLUTION	262
TRUTH AND FALSE AT A BALANCE	263

TO BE HATED FOR NOTHING	264
IN SEARCH OF GOOD	265
STEPPING ON A FEET OF INTENSE HATRED	266
RESPECT	266
WHY DO I BEHAVE LIKE THAT	268
BY GOD, I HAVE BEEN TAKEN FOR A RIDE	268
WAY TO GOOD LIFE	269
POWER AND TIMIDITY LEADS TO DISASTER	270
TALKING TO A PERSON WITH WEIRD SENSIBILITY	271
THOSE WHOSE BEHAVIOR MATCH	272
LOOKING FOR GOOD	272
ARGUMENT BETWEEN AN OPTIMIST AND A PESSIMIST	273
OPERATING BELOW ZERO	274
SOLUTION FOR THE MOST SHAMEFUL VICES	274
LUCKY AND UNLUCKY	275
UNIVERSAL DONOR VERSUS UNIVERSAL RECIPIENT	276
IF YOU WANT TO LIVE HAPPY	277
THE EFFECT OF CORRUPTION	278
SEEKING ADVICE	279
FIRE SAFES	280
AVARICE	281
GUESS WHO I AM	282
COOPERATION	283
THE VALUE ONE GIVES TO HIMSELF	284
COLD HATRED	285
A COWARD	286
ENEMY POSING AS A FRIEND	287
RELATION BETWEEN STYLE OF LIVING AND DEATH	288
WORLD WITHOUT MARRIAGE	288
MARRIAGE	289
POWER, RICHES AND PRIDE	289
TELLING TRUTH	290

NATURE IN LIFE & POEMS

TELLING FALSE	291
PERSONALITY CLASH	291
FELLOW HUMAN A DOUBLE-EDGED SWORD	292
KNOW THIS FACT SO FIRMLY	292
THE ADVICE OF GRAND MA FISH (I)	293
THE ADVICE OF GRAND MA FISH (II)	294
WHEN IT IS TOO DARK	296
WHO ARE THE WORST ENEMIES	296
AN EXEMPLARY SCHOLAR	297
A THIEF LIKES AND DISLIKES	297
SAY AND DO	298
WHEN NIGHT IS LONGER THAN DAY	299
WHEN DAY IS LONGER THAN NIGHT	299
WHEN YOU FEEL BETRAYED	300
LOVE AND HATRED	301
GOOD AND BAD LUCK	301
INDIVIDUAL AND PUBLIC INTEREST	302
CHOOSING BETWEEN DIFFICULT AND EASY LIFE	303
WATCH OUT FOR GREAT EVENT	303
THINGS AND THEIR VALUES	304
COMFORT AND DANGER ARE NEIGHBORS	305
THE GREATEST AND WORST OF THINGS	305
CONSEQUENCES OF FEAR	306
GATES OF RICHES	307
THINGS AND THEIR OPPOSITES	307
CRYING IN THE WILDERNESS FOR HELP	308
WHO DOES NOT HAVE ENEMIES	309
YESTERDAY A GIRL TODAY A WOMAN	310
TRUTH AND LIE UNDER DICTATORSHIP	310
WHY EDUCATION IS IMPORTANT	311
TOO MUCH FEAR	312
NEPOTISM	313

WHETHER TO HAVE A GRAVE OR A PLACE	314
THE MOTHER OF INTEGRITY IS DEAD	314
INTELLECTUAL	315
PRICE FOR DECEPTION	316
GOOD BYE SUN	317
TYPES OF INJUSTICE	318
BELOW THE CAUSES FOR MISUNDERSTANDING	319
DOING WRONG	320
TARGET OF CONSPIRACY	321
VICTIMS OF INDIRECT CAUSES	322
WHAT HURTS MOST	322
CONFRONTING AN OPPONENT	323
TO THE ISLAND OF NO RETURN	324
ALCOHOL EFFECT	325
INJUSTICE IS UNCONQUERABLE	326
THE ROLE OF MONEY	326
CHAPTER III: NATURE AND ITS FEATURES	329
THE CAUSE THAT HAS NO CAUSE	329
A BRIDGE OF KNOWLEDGE	330
GOOD AND BAD	330
RELIGION	331
MILK	332
SLEEP AND DEATH	332
JOURNEY FROM INFINITY AND BACK	333
LIFE IS A DREAM	334
WHAT ARE WE?	335
WHERE IS MY TIME DAD?	336
ROADS OF LIFE	336
BEGINNING AND END	337
TASTES OF LIFE	338
LOOP OF LIFE	338

NATURE IN LIFE & POEMS

FOOD	339
OUR COMMON NATURE VERSUS OUR ARTIFICIAL CONCOCTION	339
LIFE AMONG STARS	340
FORCES OF LIFE	341
SEEDS	341
CHILDHOOD	342
CHILDHOOD AND ADULTHOOD AT A BALANCE	342
COMPONENT OF CONSCIOUSNESS AT A BALANCE	343
LIFE AFTER SEVENTY	344
ALL STAGES OF LIFE ARE WITH PROS AND CONS	345
IN A DRILL WITH WILD ANIMALS (JOHN'S EXPERIENCE) (I)	345
IN A DRILL WITH WILD ANIMALS (JOHN'S EXPERIENCE) (II)	346
HIV/AIDS	347
TREADING A MIDDLE PATH	347
YOUTH	348
LIFE WITHOUT DEMAND AND SUPPLY	349
PROSECUTION OF MR. SCIENCE(S) BY MR. RELIGION (R)	349
REUNION WITH ANCESTORS	350
TWO LEGS OF LIFE	351
LIFE AND HER TWO CHILDREN	351
REQUEST FOR A JOURNEY TO ETERNITY AND BACK	352
REPENTANCE COMPLAINING TO ALMIGHTY	353
I BELIEVE IN GOD MY CREATOR	354
WHETHER MOTHER NATURE IS GOOD OR BAD	355
EXPLOITS OF NATURE	356
BIRTH AND DEATH	356
BEHAVIOR OF LIFE	357
JOURNEY TO PEACE	357

HEAVEN AND HELL ARE WITHIN US	358
DAYS ARE GONE AND OLD AGE IS BORN	359
ORDER AND DISORDER	360
PROPHETS ARE ALWAYS RIGHT	361
HYENA PRAYERS	362
CHAPTER IV: POWER AND INSTITUTIONS OF POLITICS	365
THICK SKIN	365
REAL PEACE COMES AFTER DEATH	366
IN A LION KING DEN (THE HIDDEN AGENDA)	377
POWER SHARING (A DIALOGUE BETWEEN MR. LITTLE MIND AND MR. BIG MIND)	368
CRIMINAL	369
DILLEMA IN HANDLING STRONG ENEMIES	369
CONFLICT	370
DIALOGUE BETWEEN MR. PEACE AND MR. WAR	371
EFFIGY OF INJUSTICE	372
THE PRINCIPLED PERSONALITY	372
THE UNPRINCIPLED PERSONALITY	373
MASTER OF ILL INTENTIONS	374
UNITY AND HYPOCRISY	374
WHEN THEFT CEASES TO BE A CRIME	375
LIBERATION FROM PROBLEMS	375
CONSEQUENCES OF DEFEAT	376
CONSEQUENCES OF VICTORY	377
DECLARED AND HIDDEN ENEMIES	377
YOU HAVE A REASON TO WORRY	378
PRINCIPLED VERSUS OPPORTUNIST	378
INJUSTICE IS IMMORTAL	379
ORDINARY CITIZEN DILEMMA	380
DIALOGUE BETWEEN MR. KNOW-HOW AND MR. INFERIORITY COMPLEX	381

ORDERS AND RESULTS	382
PHYSICAL FORCE VERSUS WISDOM	383
LEADERS ARE DIFFERENT	383
THE MAKING OF A DICTATOR OR DEMOCRAT	384
DEMOCRACY AT THE BALANCE	385
POLITICS ARE COMPLICATED	385
HANDS OF A LEADER	386
FEELING INSECURE	387
WAR AGAINST INJUSTICE	388
COUNTRY	389
TWO BIRTHS OF A NATION	390
ENTERING DARKNESS AND VICE VERSA	391
INJUSTICE IN FRANK DISCOURSE	391
ALMIGHTY IS NOT MEDIOCRE	392
UNCOVERING THE VILE	393
WHETHER TO SUPPORT A CAUSE OR NOT	394
WHEN WRONG BECOMES RIGHT	394
YOU WILL BE HISTORY YOURSELF	395
FRIENDSHIP AND POLITICS	396
FIGHTING LION SHADOW	396
SECURITY	397
MOVING TOWARDS A BOTTOMLESS PIT	398
LIGHT WHERE ARE YOU?	399
WHEN FROGS SUDDENLY STOP CROAKING	400
PRISON WALL OF HUMAN BEINGS	401
GRID SYSTEM IN TURMOIL	401
JACK OF TWO TRADES	403
CHASING WINDS	404
WOLF IN A SHEEP CLOTH	404
SEARCH FOR HIS MAJESTY THE FREEDOM	405
PERCEPTION OF INJUSTICE	407
CONSEQUENCES OF POWER AND WEAKNESS	408

SERVITUDE AND FREEDOM	409
NEED FOR CHANGE	410
LAMENT OF MY COUNTRY	411
MISSING A TARGET	412
WE ARE IN A BOAT	413
BETWEEN SLEEP AND AWAKE	414
MR. KNOWLEDGE AND MR. POWER	415
DOUBLE PERSONALITY	515
KIDNAPPED	416
A HOUSE ON A HEAP OF SAND	417
TAKING RIGHT AND WRONG DECISIONS	418
A TREE WITH WEAK ROOTS	418
FIGHTING FOR FREEDOM	419
WAR AND PEACE	420
THE GREATEST LEADER	421
FACING LIFE CHALLENGES	422
WHEN THINGS FALL APART OR PULL CLOSE	423
DICTATORSHIP	423
DEMOCRACY AND EDUCATION	425
ROADS TO THE END CITY	426
THE GREATEST FOLLY	426
CHAPTER V: MISCELLANEOUS	429
WORLD IS FOR GOOD MANAGERS	429
AT CROSS ROADS WHAT DO I DO?	430
ARTISTS	430
SELF EMPLOYED	431
MANAGEMENT	432
A DISH OF WALWAL	432
POETRY	433
ALCOHOLISM	433
EDUCATED AND NON EDUCATED	434

THINGS TO PRAY AND NOT TO PRAY FOR	435
APPRECIATION OF THINGS FROM DISTANCE	435
CULTURE	436
A SATISFACTORY JOB	436
WHAT A DILEMMA	437
MY FOLKLORE DANCE	437
UNIVERSITY	438
ROAD	439
MUSIC	439
RAT AND ALCOHOL	440
SPOON	440
PLATE	441
TORCH	442
AN AXE	442
HOE	443
HOSPITAL	443
A STRANGE DREAM IN DEED	444
SPEED	445
GREATNESS THAT DISAPPEARED WITH A DREAM (I)	445
GREATNESS THAT DISAPPEARED WITH A DREAM (II)	446
A DREAM THAT PAID OFF	447
SEARCHING THE SAGE'S MIND	449
HISTORY PROVIDES BRICKS	450
PLAN AND ITS EXECUTION	451

ACKNOWLEDGMENT

In memoriam of our late father, Dr Bellario Ahoy Ngong Geng, this book titled Nature and Life in Poems is a monument to his passion for poetry and literary works. Our late father had a keen interest in sharing life experiences through poetry and this is a continuation of such thoughtful works by remembering and honoring him.

We offer our heartfelt thanks to the many friends of our late father, his colleagues throughout his professional life, well-wishers and the government of South Sudan who provided emotional and practical support throughout his life and through the difficult times the family experienced after his death.

Our late father was a family-oriented man who cared much about his immediate family and relatives. We dedicate his work to the entire Ngong Geng family, including wives and all their children, and his brothers and sisters who provided a source of comfort, wisdom, and immeasurable support during the times of writing these poems.

Special thanks go to Dr Luka Biong Deng who provided advice on the publication of this book. Importantly, we would like to express our many thanks to Africa World Books for editing and publishing this book. Our appreciation also goes to Dr Sara Maher, the editor, for all her effort and kindness and thanks to Peter Lual Deng of Africa World Books for all his support and facilitation in realizing the publication of this book.

To those who helped in any way, your contribution to the late Dr Bellario Ahoy Ngong Geng's family is much appreciated. As it would be impossible to mention everyone individually, please accept this acknowledgment as an expression of our deepest gratitude.

- Family of the Late Dr Bellario Ahoy Ngong

PREFACE

From an early age I enjoyed songs, statements and phrases embedded with wisdom from people. Although I'm also fond of Science disciplines, this interest grew with me. I was destined to take the line of the Arts as my profession, if it was not because of an ill-fated incident that forced on me a turning point. While I was about to choose the specialization subjects at the semi-final at secondary school in 1970, news came that my beloved Father had died of diarrhoea and soon after, my dear Moth, whom we depended on for upkeep, lost her sight from bilateral cataracts. Both are preventable ailments that could have been managed if there were skilled personnel with health knowledge in the vicinity. I immediately changed my choice in favor of Science subjects with the aim of taking medical medical studies to avenge my parents.

Still carrying forward my interest, I continued to study Art subjects and especially poems at my leisure. I enjoyed reading poems from the Academy of American Poets which I found on the internet and when I came across those ones from Africa my interest was much elevated. Some of those that I read included the books entitled "Building the nation and other poems" by Henry Barlow, from Uganda and "Poems from East Africa" by David Cook and David Rubadiri. They finally influenced me to embrace poetry.

The last drop that made "the glass over flow" in May 2010, was when the Nationwide advertisement invited interested applicants to write the National Anthem in poem form for the soon to be new born nation of South Sudan. Although I did not send my poems for the competition's scrutiny, being shy to expose my weakness, that one triggered in me an urge to write on any interesting event that came across my mind in poems. It was first a leisure time-spending exercise but when I was able to accomplish 50 poems, I thought of embarking on an ambitious project of 1001 poems.

Later on I felt I was swimming in an ocean with no shore insight and it would be better to test the waters first by organizing those I had finished into a booket (Part l) with a plan to add other booklets in a space of time to meet the size of the project. That is how this first print entitled "NATURE AND LIFE IN POEMS-PART (I)" came into being. "NATURE AND LIFE IN POEMS-PART (ll)" is number two in the series.

Note from Publisher:
The decision to posthumously publish PARTS l & ll as one book was made by Dr Bellario's family. Chapter l contains auto-biographic poems. In both PARTS l & ll, Chapters 2-5, have the same titles and numbering but the poems are different.

INTRODUCTION

These poems serve two purposes. One, they are for entertainment as some poems carry with them humorous expressions and most of lines in many stanzas enjoy a musical, rhythmical ending. The other purpose and the most important is; they are impregnated with a message intended either to raise the status of an object or a subject or praise nature and its features. Examples of these are found in many of them such as in the poems of Chapter 1: No 1 *"Aweil"* or No 5 and 6, in praising *"My First Teacher"* Dominic Matong. The message may be carrying a problem or a solution as you will see in:

Part l:
Poem No. 39 on *"Corruption I"*, No. 50 on how to obtain *"Wealth II"*, No. 137 and 138 on *"Passing through a Hole of a Needle"*. Or it may be an exposure of a problem without necessarily offering a solution such as in poems No. 125 and 126 *"The Young Generation"*.

In all, these poems are either expressed using direct phrases, as most of them are, or presented as a dialogue between two characters as in No. 99 *"Dialogue between Well to do and Less to* do", No. 241 *"Good and a Bad ruler"* and No. 248 *"Dialogue between Mr. Inquisitive and Mr. Freedom Fighter"*. In some cases they are presented as soliloquies such as in No. 279 *"On Defense of Political Naivety"* and No. 281/282 *"Freedom in Focus"*. They are also organized in regular stanzas of 3 or more depending on the size of the subject matter to be addressed in the poem. Each stanza represents a logical idea or concept. It is either a continuation of the previous idea or offering a contrast or a conclusion.

Part ll:

Poems in Part ll may also be carrying a solution or a problem such as in the poem No. 62 *"In search of Good"*, No. 64, *"Respect"* and No. 77 *"If You Want to Live Happy"*. It may be an exposure of a problem without necessarily offering a solution, such as in poems No. 78, the *"Effect of Corruption"* and No. 79 *"Seeking Advice"*, No. 196 in "the *"Effigy of Injustice"*. It may be criticizing or ridiculing a phenomenon or a subject in a satirical fashion as in poems No. 172*"Reunion with Ancestors"*, No. 175 *"Request for a Journey to Eternity and Back"* and No. 176 *"Repentance Complaining to Almighty"*.

In all, these poems are either expressed using direct phrases as most of them are or presented as a dialogue between two characters as in No. 191 *"Power Sharing"*, No. 236 *"Good and a Bad Ruler"*, No. 243 *"Dialogue between Inquisitive and Mr. Freedom Fighter"*, No. 371 *"Know-how and Inferiority Complex"* and in some cases as soliloquies such as in No. 183 *"Heaven and Hell are Within Us"*, or as monologues as in poems No. 168 *"Treading a Middle Path"* and No. 133 *"Target of Conspiracy"*.

Chapter I: About My Self and Locality

This deals with me and location, a sort of autobiography. This entails description about the date and place of my birth; my first educational encounter; my secondary and higher education; my jobs with the Sudan Government before joining the liberation struggle; job positions within and after the freedom movement. It also includes the description of a cultural milieu from which I came from and ending with sentiments about a place dear to my heart (Kiir Adem) nowadays wallowing in a political dispute between South Sudan and Sudan.

Note from Publisher: Parts l and ll contain four chapters each. Each chapter has the same title and theme and the poems are listed in the same numerical sequence but the poems are different.

Chapter II: Relations and Behaviour

This deals with people, relations and their behaviors. It highlights reasons that make people indulge in deception and ungratefulness; ways to gain wealth, the importance of education, knowledge and health, love, hatred and friendship. It also includes the importance of close relationship within the kinship structure such as the father, the mother, siblings and grand relations. It also describes the wedge between the younger and older generations.

Chapter III: Nature and its Features

This delves into nature and its features. How beautiful and well organized it is. It starts with human nature and nature of problems and covering such features as mountains, hills, rivers and valleys as well as the heavenly bodies such as the sun; the moon and stars not forgetting the earthly fauna including cows, dogs, hens, some useful insects and some fishes. Adding beside the flora such as trees, forest and some selected trees of economic and social importance.

Chapter IV: Power and Institutions of Politics

This covers power and institutions of politics. This encompasses vast areas of governance and its institutions, nature and value of politics, making of leaders, behaviors of leaders and type of leaders, how leaders gain and loose power, their indulgences, etc. It also exposes freedom, together with the essence and fate of liberation, types of political solutions, justice, Law and Courts, types of prisons and public service versus private service.

Chapter V: Miscellaneous

This embodies miscellaneous. These are topics that could not be classified under the heading chapters above and some of them even though they deal with one issue are not enough to constitute a chapter of its own. What is common in all these chapters is the fact that they cover natural features and issues we meet in everyday life. I do not at all claim that they are not known. What I have merely done is to enliven them.

CHAPTER I

ABOUT MY SELF AND LOCALITY

1. AWEIL

Where ever we are, from you we hailed
When you are in jail
We feel a sense of guilt
And immediately arrange a bail

You are a duck
That produces golden eggs
To all of us you distributed your cakes
Back from the mission you welcome us with a hug

You deserve a pat on the back
If we had tails, we would strongly wag
And put on you a golden tag
To dangle along your neck

THE YEAR OF MY BIRTH (1951)

Parents were not explicit of the date
Because they were illiterate
But they could make a clever estimate
That almost concluded the debate

In 1952, when the sun in February eclipsed
The breast of the mother was held by my lips
Having been born when gifts
 Of season were getting ready before the year slipped

Interpreted by men of pen
I had six months gain
 Before our location had briefly forsaken the sun
The time was August nineteen fifty one

LOCATION SPOT OF MY BIRTH

I was born in Thur Ariath
Where I took my first breath
Compared to other areas
It was full of reeds

It is traversed by River Kuom
And a wet season stream
In dry season, it is warm
While in May the rainy clouds loom

If ever you approach Tiaraliet
At the bosom of area called Paliet

Follow the north direction on the road
11 kms, right of the road is the site

MY FIRST SCHOOL (1959)

My first school in 1959, was at Malek-Alel
Situated on the iron stone plateau called "Alel"
A distance south of River Lol
All along in a war but recently received a lull

How wonderful to learn my first alphabets
It was very difficult, I bet
I had a second thought to quit
But rescinded after singing beautiful Roberts

How valuable my first letter characters
After I have received my lectures
And encouragement from teachers
I dreamed to be a Doctor

MY FIRST TEACHER (I)

Oh! Torch of my light
My mouth remains tight
Not knowing how to thank you right
For opening my sight
To fly with a kite

You were my bridge
I crossed to knowledge rich

Those were days passed away hurriedly
When I used to sip hot porridge
And kept tumbling down when lining a ridge

Oh! Developer of my personal esteem
You showed me the systems
And how to work in teams
And inculcated in me our customs
Which I usually adore with costumes

MY FIRST TEACHER (II)

Dominic Matong
When I was brought to you young
You never inquired which tribe I belonged
In the course of training my tongue
You never hesitated to correct my wrong

Dominic Matong
I recalled your aspiring songs
They were not too long
But deep to my bone they banged
To stir up nationalism from within

Dominic Matong
That time I thought I was playing with cow dung
And your instructions like ping pong
Now I realized you were a gong
Alerting me to escape the beast fangs

MY INTERMEDIATE SCHOOL (1963-1964)

My middle grade school was in Aweil
Where the spirits of my ancestors dwell
Through it passes the rail
Bringing all the needs for sale

Teaching was marvelous
It produced well seasoned fellows
That later made up national zealots
Other schools were jealous

The credit goes to Mr. George Wuhib
As a Head master, he was a hub
Around whom the school raised hope
And contributed to what it reaped

SUNDAY STRIKE OF 1964

When Friday was imposed
By Khartoum Government by then
Southern students raised an angry voice
Preferring Sunday at any cost
And schools were closed

Three years I spent at home
At the bosom of my Mom
Enjoying home education and game
To carry forward her name

Educators were making a place hunt
A suitable place was found
All target children from the South joined
At last it was launched
In 1967, I resumed school at Tonj

MY SECONDARY SCHOOL (1969)

After results were out successful
Our friends invited us to dine
How they were so kind!
I joined Rumbek in nineteen sixty nine

My secondary school in name was in Rumbek
But due to war we were in Omdurman in fact
After running away from the zone of yoke
Competition in Rumbek was neck to neck

Studies were multipurpose
Though more on academic courses
With strong leadership from our boss
Every student that was there rose

MY MEDICAL STUDIES IN ALEXANDRIA (1973)

I joined it in nineteen seventy three
At first I entertained some worry
But everything was not to vary
Medical studies were Arabic free

Six years were not long
Like between a nose and a lung
As on our studies we hanged
And emerged learned and still young

Grateful to who made our studies possible
Assessing players on the crucible
Sudanese officials made it feasible
While Egyptian role was too visible

WORKING AS AN INTERN (1980)

The location was Khartoum North hospital
They say it was vital
To add in total
What I gathered a little

I was to complete four domains
As the subjects mains
That was to conclude my gains
As the assignment came to the end

That period was a must
Never cause a fuss
As one is not allowed to practice first
Before passing that stage

POSTED TO WAU HOSPITAL (1981)

In Wau, I had my first post
That was assigned by boss
The work was devouring up to my nose
For six months I had to roast

Taking rounds in four wards
And prescribing in all cards
Was to be my stick yard
In addition to keep alert

My boss had to render a report
To effect that I was on board
In order to prevent torts
In law courts

TWO YEARS AT GOGRIAL HOSPITAL (1981-83)

End nineteen eighty one
I was there at hand
Having been certified to run
The hospital alone

How challenging it was
To work like bees
And ran a risk
To bring diseases to their knees

How relieving
To see a patient peacefully sleeping

And face beaming with smile
After it had been distorted with pain

TWO YEARS AT AWEIL HOSPITAL (1983-85)

My heart throbbed as I arrived to the town
It was twelve years since I disowned
And it had grown a bit from what was known
But alas! Good times were fast sinking down
As the second war of 1983 was on the horizon

When afternoons came around
News were full of name John
How many days to count
Before the doom day dawned
We were counting nervously alone

Then the day came galloping at dawn
All available weapons were to sound
I heard a step on the lawn
It was a summon of duty bound
Because the number of wounded victims had grown

POST GRADUATE IN KHARTOUM (1986-88)

The year was nineteen eighty six
The studies for two years were fixed
The chickens had already laid eggs
It was for me to crack the chicks

My patient was a community
Clean environment breeds purity
While dirty environment brings perplexity
That must be controlled with much dexterity

During the war, how valuable were those studies
Cholera would have stricken mothers and daddies
Scattered everywhere would have been their bodies
The happiest would have been the enemies

WITH CARE INTERNATIONAL AT NAHUD (1988)

1988 was the year
The war had intensified so far
And because of fear
Homes were left at the rear

People left land so dear
And with nothing to eat and wear
They came to look for care
As the conditions were dire

CARE was there
To people complaints they tended to hear
The organization was so sincere
To lend their ears

AT THE MINISTRY OF HEALTH IN KHARTOUM (1989)

My post was Deputy Director
Malaria control was my assignment
NGOS were my oar
To strike in depth at malaria's core

Things were not to be cheese and honey
Relations with Administrator were thorny
Because he was a power pony
I was subjected to fear and agony

The Director reactions were funny
In the other they were canny
To placate me I was offered a course with money
And in no time I was there with brother Wani

MALARIA COURSE IN THAILAND AND ITALY (1990)

The year was nineteen ninety
In the country, there was a new power giant
Its first enemy was wine
And people of other faiths in line

In the morning, I prayed for I might not dine
At night I hid for I might not see the day light
Young against their will were driven to fight
For GOD sake they had to die in order to bring might

Those were days I went on a course
It was like going to Mars

Where I could not hear lion roars
Still when I returned the situation had not reversed

JOINING SPLM IN 1990

When the course ended in Italy
I made my mind without feeling jittery
Ordering my body and mind to tally
And joined the Movement for injustices I had endured bitterly

At last I was in Addis
Among all cities
I felt I was the safest
After escaping the sadists

Next destination was the Sudan bush
The forests were very huge
Nevertheless we had to push
In order to liberate the land of Cush

MILITARY TRAINING IN 1991

As it was forever body requirement by then
One has to drop a hoe or a pen
And join military training without rant
To end when acquiring a gun

The duration was six months
But interrupted by Ethiopian menace
Ammunitions fired were in tons
We had to escape to be in tune

Catastrophes were in the series run
Nasir group were to away turn
And enemy threat was on our trail hunt
The situation looked like a U turn

POSTED TO KAPOETA (1991)

In August 1991, I came to Kapoeta
Nasir coup was brewing, I had no iota
A colleague in Kapoeta was driven by a current of water
In his place, I was assigned to manage the roster

As time went by
I learned he had joined the guys
And I were there to stay
To witness brothers die

In that year, I watched Kapoeta fall
And we heard Torit knelt
As Yirol and Bor melted
The nearest to us was hell

COMMISSIONED CAPTAIN IN 1992

We were summoned to the officers' shade
Where the lunch was made
After we ate
We were informed of the date

That morning we stood in a parade
We saw soldiers, to our direction hurried
We thought we had a raid
Bu that was C-in-C entering the gate

We stood erect as statues in rain
The names were read as we stood in line
Each was given as records contained
I was commissioned as a captain number nine

SURGEON IN ASHWA HOSPITAL (1992)

On retreat from Torit
Our move with patients to Ashwa was hurried
To avoid being caught by war current
That was approaching to launch a raid

As we received more wounded guys
Operations increased in size
We had to make more ties
To keep services nice

Ashwa was a white spot in the middle of darkness
Stuffed with all the medical niceties from the west
All surgical interventions were the best
Available at the base

POSTED TO MUNDRI (1992)

Mundri was another front to the West
Beside others, the health situation was in a mess
Work was to go around the clock without rest
The food was there but had no taste

One day we had a visit from a foe
It was a surprise visit, no one knew
The farmer in the field saw
Surprised, he hurt his toe

They advanced in columns and rows
All in the thick grass in bow
Hoodoo! We let the cows go
And ordered the lions to open their jaws

POSTED TO AKON IN 1993

Further to northwest was Akon
Its lofty Abyei tree was the beacon
Like the praying deacon
Akon those days was a resistance icon

Along the railway on that fateful day
The first encounter was in May
On the road the ambush lay
And we had martyrs pay

On the door I sensed a knock
And heard people talk

What I saw made me shocked
But that was a way of unlocking the yoke

AS HEALTH COORDINATOR FOR NORTHERN BHAR-EL-GHAZAL (1994)

As enemy was harassing
Health needs were pressing
There was need of addressing
 Before becoming embarrassing

SRRA posted me to the region
I was to work behind our legions
It was more or less like a dungeon
But it was a mission to liberate our nation

Following us were herds of falcons
I thought they were enjoying the season
Instead they were on a mission
To clean up our remains destroyed by weapons

HEALTH COORDINATOR FOR SPLM AREAS (1998)

On my desk there was a radio message
I thought it was written by a sage
For at the end it was concluded by a wise adage
All qualities of a post were there except a wage

The message was from the SRRA head
In his office he offered me a seat

And talked a lot about the need
Which he thought I was fit to meet

They called it a promotion
Because the work was huge as an ocean
With all my devotion
I had to be paid with a bag of ration

A DELEGATE TO CPA TALKS (2003)

In 2003 I joined the CPA talks
They were as hard as rock
We had to adopt patience of a watch dog
As an axe to break the yoke

Wisdom justifies the means
One simple strategy brought great gains
We had to present hard options
In order to get what we yearned

The architect of the idea was Dr. John
He taught us to be persistently keen
Even though bitten and soaked by rains
Otherwise all efforts would have been in vain

AS COMMISIONER OF SRRC (2005)

SRRC was a relief wing of the Movement
The one Institution that had resources at hand
In 2005 I was appointed to head that giant
Facing challenge I went

The task was to have people repatriated
Had them aided
Then rehabilitated
In place they were related

It was not an easy task
Work was to be done from dawn to dusk
A peaceful sleep only masked
What would in the day becomes dust

CHAIRPERSON OF HIV/AIDS COMMISSION, 2006

As the human war ended
The virus war ascended
The strategies had to be amended
To the goals intended

Our first task to muster
Was to establish a war machine
After allaying fears of Bashir
That it was not a war veneer

The effective weapons were three
Taking the first two, you are a saint on a tree
Taking the last one alone, you are in a hurry
And taking them all, you are free

GENTLEMAN OF TIARALIET (I)

When in April thunderstorms roar
Heralding the approach of rain showers
The gentleman sets cultivation on course
Ready to finish a farm before other chores

He works from when dawn tears
To when dusk lurks
Singing his favorites in a voice with pitch albeit hoarse
To prevent boring courses

He hurriedly knocks at a cattle camp doors
Where milk in gourd jars
Awaiting him to quench his hunger force
It is to be a number of days before his body swells

GENTLEMAN OF TIARALIET (II)

In the middle of summer fall
When grass is tall
And crops are nearing yield
He comes back with a body like a ball

An impact of cow milk he consumed
To enable him win fattening competition spell
That was a yearly cultural call
Soon after he was again by his home wall

Enjoying a new harvest with palls
In that season every group has a role

Women have the produce to sell
And men play void and null

GENTLEMAN OF TIARALIET (III)

Dry season arrives
Lack of water threatens all lives
The gentleman has no choice but to have cattle on a drive
To where they can survive

Nearest is upstream on land of Jur tribe
Where bees in abundance on beehives thrive
The stuff of honey derived
Will vary up gentlemen diet of various types

When he has spent months not less than five
And when clouds on the sky gathered to ripe
He will signal going back by blowing his horn pipe
Hastening home to see his future wife

LADY OF TIARALIET

She gets up at dawn
To sweep home compound of their own
Then she milks cows and releasing them to a lawn
And prepares a day meal using home grown
Before she goes to buy more needs from village town

At the way back home
She would fetch firewood bundles for Mom

To make a meal flame
Food must be ready before hyenas roam
There after she joins folklore dances

That is where she can arrange dates
With determinants of her fate
To those lovely mates
She will open gate
Leaving the hesitant to wait

MILE 14 (KIIR ADEM)

Mile 14 my daughter my own
You are a product of my groin
At my bosom you have grown
Until you approach fourteen
Just before ready to produce grain

When they have seen you beautiful
They want to marry you off to awful
The one from frogs and owls
My daughter to kiss a frog in a pool
That can only be accepted by a fool

No, to your uncles, No
They will do that lo!
When my eyes are closed with my jaw
Ears permanently deaf to even a dove coo
And never aware to all woes

PART I
CHAPTER II

RELATIONS AND BEHAVIOUR

HOW EASILY YOU CAN FORGET

Once you complained, winced and twisted
As your rights were violated and inverted
With sympathy your friends were tormented
As you looked behind you were comforted

At a flash you overcame the difficulty
Flying with bliss you defy the gravity
Kicking left and right with impunity
Mercilessly violating others with ferocity

How easily you can forget
The time you were a target

Although you are not any longer worried
You will remain haunted
By the shadows of your victims

KINGDOM OF UNGRATEFULNESS

I'm King GODWILL
From the Kingdom I hailed
I select my servants at will
And discharge them as well

As I'm million times worth
Diligence, must I be served with
To avoid my firestorm wrath
That must be delivered with rage

Expect your services to be rewarded less
For other people needs are worthless
As they are weightless
In my Kingdom of ungratefulness

TAKEN FOR A RIDE

Hare you are the only choice we have
To run a race of our destiny brave
Prepare yourself for a day engraved
When the King will fulfill the promise he gave

That day came for a race to be set up
Activities were similar to that of beehives

The preparations were made by a club
Already the hare was conjuring up a cup
At D-DAY there was no hare in the race
But the tortoise was soaked with praise
Miraculously the hare name was erased
By the King, the giver of grace

CORRUPTION (I)

Confronting your foe
Your tactics are two
In one you bow
And in the other you paw

In both you are victorious
Walking away decorous
And the enemy delirious
Licking its wounds in continuous

You burrow deep
Rendering economy dwarf
Making few to boom
And majority doomed

How mighty you are
Chameleon you pair
On search your enemy err
As you cannot be there

In a duel you capture the enemy mind
In its pocket you enter mild

And up the stomach in extra mile
As you conclude the game in might
Flexibility you are capable
In one aspect you are incalculable
In other you are invisible
Making confrontation impossible

In hot pursuit you brandish a weapon
Of late you have acquired ammunitions
Targeting your enemy with elimination
Which you do sometimes with precision

Under your blows the enemy suffer
Their efforts torn asunder
While people watch in surrender
With your posture they can't temper

Cure cannot be a solution
As you fight to prevent humiliation
There can be one option
Remedy can be on prevention.

CORRUPTION (II) *(Neck and Head disease)*

Come here folks of my country
Converge under a Doctor's tree
And learn about corruption killing spree
And why it cannot be made to flee

This is how a Doctor teaches without fees
Corruption is like a disease

Like many diseases listed
Some body parts are affected with ease

Neck and head are the victims it seizes
Making it difficult for the rest to resist
Never allow your country to slide to abyss
Like AIDS it has no cure even if you insist

CORRUPTION ON DEFENSIVE

Corruption! Corruption! Corruption!
You always call my name with a frown
As if you do not know me in perfection
How I came and how I exist in this world
If you did not attend my coronation
Take my biography in this brief presentation

I was born when you shunned my cousin anarchy
Where robbery was the practice of the day
And established instead ostensibly
The so called government entity
Where all resources are put in the hands solely
Of few humans called leaders to determine destiny

Being accessible to wealth of the people
Natural logic is ever able
To command that they must satisfy their selves triple
Before they satisfy others double
By giving forth an offspring capable
Called Corruption (My dear self) crowned with apple

If you doubt this then search the birth register at your station
Of the ordinary persons without responsibility portion
Whether you will find an offspring with name Corruption
I bet to pay you one million
Of hard currency to your account bastion

You have two options to choose from only
Instead of crying foul of my name carelessly
Every time I go for a walk leisurely
Either you bring back again anarchy
And its offspring robbery

Or you raise me up like a sail
And seat me in a golden throne firmly nailed
Sometimes it is better to kiss a frog tamed in a pail
With bulging eyes and belly happily waving a hand
Than a scorpion with a stinging tail

CORRUPT PERSONALITY VERSUS FAIR PERSONALITY

The so called fair personality crop
Call me Corrupt
Because they envy my wealth stuff
What is fair about them to adopt?
While they are not fair to themselves enough

As for me I'm fair like a dove
That is why I'm at the top
I do not get it by stealing cobs
But by getting my share of loaf
From public garden crop

Whether I get more than my share
Cannot be a cause to fight
Because I'm being compelled by appetite
And who can resist the force of appetite light
Only fair personality with a foolish pride

EVERYWHERE SURROUNDED BY CORRUPTION (I)

Oh GOD saves my soul!
This is my last call
This is how I have watched it unfold
I resigned my position in the public sector roll
Because Mr. Corruption denied me my meal
Horribly his corruption behavior was taking toll
I used to miss my monthly pay all
Because I did not fulfill my role
Of contributing to educate his girl

Hoping that I shall get respite
I joined the business sector
When I knocked the door and waited
To my surprise it was opened wide
By Mr. Corruption!
He ushered me inside
Provided hot drinks and some snacks to bite
And inquired straight
If he could render any service to my delight

I dashed back in confusion
But I thought of sector for information
As I'm on notification

It exposes every bit of correct communication
And since facts cannot lie in bed with Corruption
He cannot dwell there with satisfaction
When I presented my complaint for publication
Corruption was there in preparation
To audit my article in question!

EVERYWHERE SURROUNDED BY CORRUPTION (II)

I escaped in horror
And quitting my ideas to become a warrior
Because of its associated acts of terror
I resorted to judiciary order
With hope to judge better
My case with Mr. Corruption
On the appointed date by a caller
I found Mr. Corruption himself erecting a barrier
Preventing unwanted as he has become the case judge!

Battered and disillusioned to the full
I turned to the last resort weary and doubtful
I joined the Faith pool
Where people supposed to be faithful
Do detest corruption as a rule
As it is related to evil
When the door was openly pulled
Presiding was Mr. Corruption dressing colorful
And leading Prayers of the hopeful!

I suddenly pulled back on time
Exhausted, weak and poor, I was left with a dime

My right and means to achieve it never rhyme
Greatly losing hope but who to blame
As Mr. Corruption soaked in crime
Has rendered the world lame
In few minutes to come you will hear my voice frail
I plead for your angels to receive me on climb
Bye, bye, Mr. Corruption has triumphed

I'M INNOCENT

Down, down, You ungrateful in chief!
Don't you consider the service without break?
I have rendered to this country without sleep
Even to the expense of my life trip
Yet you have the temerity to climb a cliff
And call me a thief?

Wealth squandered out?
What is this wealth you are talking about?
How would you have this wealth I doubt?
Would you? As you are weak and a coward
Rescue it from robber's port
If I did not tower the crowd

Nonsense you have accused me for nothing mister
Natural justice demands that
If one has rescued a property stolen by a robber
He should pay himself some dollars fewer
Before giving balance to the owner
If ever there is any left over

TEMPLE OF MY KINDNESS

When I follow you
They thought I was going to a loo
If like them I make a boo
You will drag me to a zoo

With kindness comes tameness
Leading to peace and progress
Lack of it is distress
A nephew of rudeness

If kindness disappears in horror
And comes in place the terror
The humankind will be in uproar
Because of few in error

TREE TOP

Tree top was reserved for exceptional those
In their place inexperienced and young rose
As the competition goes
On the ground the elderly dozed

The tree will preserve no seeds
And the leaves will drop with ease
The growth of the trunk will cease
As it will only accommodate bees

This is called treason
Since the tree is threatened with no apparent reason

With elderly trodden and plunged to isolation
By their offspring in rebellion

THE HARDWORK REWARD

Folks of my kith and kin
Searching for lives and wins
Avoiding corruption and sins
Packing everything repugnant in bins

You need to toil and sweat
In order to get it sweet
Keep your feet wet
As you remove weeds

Rest assure your day
So profuse with ray
As you remove hay
From produce of rye

WEALTH (I)

The ways of acquiring you are three
By inheritance when luck sets the gates free
Through extortion when law is hung by a decree
Nobly when hard work and luck agree

Effect on your subjects is in three folds
You pamper them not to fall
You raise them to value of gold
And make them live near hell

Wealth for its sake is good
But knowledge acts as its food
As plant has a root
To nourish its shoots

Wealth (II)
Here is how I'm obtained
With only your labor you have me retained
Carry me first on your shoulders as pillars sustain
And keep me as well as a prisoner detained

Later I carry you forever as our friendship last
For with that friendship our dice is cast
Do not let it rust
As the losses will be vast

Do not tell me
You do not like me
For that will be taking tea
Infested with bees

Wealth (III)

Wealth is comfortable and powerful
As it unlocks the chains with thunderbolt
In satisfying the needs the subject is left grateful
Cementing the spouse as they spend their moon in Liverpool

Never hold it soft
As it slips out with cough

When weather is hot
Better hide it in a pot
This is the advice everyone heeds
Let the wisdom fill the head
Before wealth has a seat
To support your needs

WEALTH (IV)

Wealth starts at Zero
Above, you are in Euros and a hero
Below you are to borrow
Until you strike a bone marrow

It is your choice to decide what to be
If you want riches you need to pay a fee
Otherwise what is left for thee
Is to kiss a ground with a knee

Never quiver
For with that the poverty runs deeper
In this world there is no giver
That can ever give without shiver

JUSTICE

Justice prevails among those of equal power
Even though they are always fewer
They control the majority weak and poorer
Never shall equality exist between the powerful and the bower

The truth is that the strong seeps
The strength of the weak deep
So the weak gives
With nothing to reap

Strong shall never dispense rights
Without a fight
As the weak remains quiet
They keep the control tight

THE JOY OF RECEIVING

Witness the giant smile of a receiver
Overshadowing the grin of a Giver
One is a saver
And the other never

If you continue giving
To poverty you are moving
And if you continue receiving
To a beggar you are opting

Some choose to be humble
In order to live noble
And the other feeble
In order to gain double

LOVE

Love is blind outside
But has eyes inside
When the outer force pushes it aside
The inner force will place it beside

When love is intensive
The lovers never hear gossip
And when the opposition is massive
They turn deaf and passive

Lo! When the intensive love breaks
The result is the gaping crack
Although the tricks can make it drag
It can never be put back erect

LOVERS

Lovers have close vision romantic
When deep in their hearts they turn fanatic
Deeper still they border lunatics
With attempt to separate them they go nomadic

Only death can separate real lovers
Their hearts are tight with golden covers
As they live in a den made of flowers
Its doors are decorated by strings of copper

When you are out there with your pal
Try to compare everything without fail

And conclude without a jolt
Love to life is salt

GIVE THEM A PROPER NAME(I)

When a cat on their way lies
And the mice realize
To run back before sunrise
Call them wise

That was going to be disastrous
As the cat is stronger and carnivorous
Making the confrontation dangerous
For the poor mice though populous

When the enemy is stronger
And it is poised to conquer
It is wise to embrace departure
Before the game is over

GIVE THEM A PROPER NAME (II)

When they decline to move forward
To fight their equal foe leeward
Towards demanding a just reward
They are cowards

They will be damned forever
As their hopes will be realized never
Servitude and suffering their pay over
Even if they complain ever

They should confront the enemy headlong
As with their right their fate belong
Even when the enemy device a flank
Their resolve will take them along

GIVE THEM THE PROPER NAME (III)

As they use their torrents
To intimidate the downtrodden
Even though they run their errands
Nickname them tyrants

The consequence is humiliation
Meted out in human rights violation
There is no reason for jubilation
When human values are subject to demolition

Beware Oh! Tyrants
Although your vile descends in current
The society remains vibrant
Expecting your exit to Orient

FATE OF HUMAN VALUES
(Virtues: justice, fairness, equality, transparency, honesty)

When properly shielded as a child in uterus
They lift the human kind from ashes
And feed them out of golden dishes
Making them lofty out of desert oasis

Unfortunately leaders play but a game
As they pay lip service without shame
Virtues are not their aim
Instead they leave them maimed

In consequence people are distraught
As they are led down by the leaders they brought
Tolerating them is a cut throat
And with drawing back is a distant shout

SELFISHNESS

You are a master everyone serves
But since you are disfigured by the lameness you have
You are kept head down in a cave
Not to shame people with your ugly curve

You are shrewd in making the owner greedy
And denying the right of the needy
All the people but one deserts you pretty
Even if you offer them a treaty

There is a reason you can stay longer without regret
We hate you in open but love you in secret
In spite the negative impression we make
Deep in us you have a place in our heart

HIDDEN HATRED

Beware of hidden hatred as it bites
Because the perpetrator hides
While the victim unaware eats
Not knowing the food is infested with mites

The perpetrator intends to kill victim unaware
His tricks are not to be known anywhere
He may put a poison in your glassware
And deny his involvement as he swears

This is the most vicious vice among all
As it is better from the high you fall
Than to succumb to plots behind a wall
Undermining your desirous goal

THERE IS ALWAYS A DOOR TO OPEN

When a door is closed in front of you
Including all the other doors in row
And the ceiling lowering a yoke
While a floor is guided by a foe

There comes the feeling of despair
As this destroys hope you aspire
With no will to prepare
As the living prefers

At this juncture never surrender to your foe
Just look behind at another door as you vow

Mother Nature will open as does a hero
And you can march out with a bow

HOPE

Hope is the guide of life
As it binds husband and wife
Making the relationship ripe
So strong not to be cut with a knife

Without hope life is meaningless
As it will be aimless
Further loss will render it limbless
Rendering it lifeless

Set a target to get hope
And hang on the rope
To get to a top
With time you can cope

LUCK

Luck is gain without efforts
Some get it more than their comfort
Others have a glimpse when it departs
When going back to its depot

They feel happy and special
Out of the crowd they appeal
But anything without efforts is not real
As it evaporates in extra mile

Lucky ones are both blessed and cursed
When they get it with joy they burst
But quickly empty their purse
Since they have not worked for it to emerge

FRIEND

People of similar thoughts and opinions
Harboring the same strategies and vision
Singing the same songs with unison
Even when they climb up the mount Zion

Real ones share the same problems and joy
In supporting each other they enjoy
And in meeting difficulties they stay
Even if together they die

Bond of friendship is stronger than any bond
As it is built on free choice of their own
Let their fate get drawn
And they will meet it without moan

NEIGHBOR

Neighbor is a natural gift
Provided by God to keep
Never attempt to create a rift
For he is a pole to grip

Common challenges you share
Any trouble the first to hear
And can take risk without fare
To save the very life you consider dear

Like comfort of your bed is your neighbor
A good neighbor is a savior
A bad one is like a ship without an anchor
Endangering the life of a sailor

MOTHER

You are a channel for my creation
In your womb I lived for nine months duration
Ungratefully I caused you pain when I left for the world destination
Still you mind to care for me on your efforts to create a nation.

Your fate and mine are connected before birth
Because of me I may cause your death
And because of your bad health
I may not see the earth

You icon of tender love
Stand in line with a dove
To raise the banner of hope
No one else can do your job

FATHER

You are a conduit for my creation
When the nature on its own volition
Molded me to your admiration
And be a part of your nation

You are vital in keeping family strong
In one you are a corrector of wrong
In the other the bread winner for my survival
In addition of being a cultural patron

In all misfortunes seen
And all that run to ruin
A family without a father to lean
Is like a beehive without a queen

SON

You are a natural gift to our family
At the bosom of our love you came calmly
To meet our request timely
After we prayed humbly

A messenger of posterity
And a service provider with variety
You hold the banner with authority
Bestowed to you by eternity

Let me reveal this truth as you wait
Take this advice to your heart

While pass a message to people you meet
A family without a male heir is dead in deed

DAUGHTER

You breathing flowers
Come my dear with cheers
To wipe our eyes of tears
And deliver love without fear

Sanctuary of our family joy
All pass the days
When family chores become your toy
And sweat becomes your pay

Then comes a day of darkness
Which you replace with cheerfulness
And roughness with smoothness
A family without a daughter lacks happiness

SISTER

She shared the mother womb with me
When I had eyes to see
I realized I was not on my knee
But has companion to be

From tender age we shared family problems and joy
Learning to help each other as we play toys
And managing household chores as we welcome a day
Yet she renders extra services that lay

From what people read
And reflected from their deeds
Brothers without a sister breed
Lacks half of their needs

BROTHER

With you we shared our mother womb
Later we shared our family home
Sleeping in one family room
And shared one family comb

How beautiful those days
When we used to play with clays
Modifying it in so many ways
Under a tingling sun rays

When one is in trouble he brings cures
And when laden with grief he is an eraser
Under assault by enemies he brings pressure
A person without a brother loses half of life treasures

IF I HAVE A BROTHER

The one who shared with me one womb
And then shared with me one room
As we giggle in one home
Call him Brother Tom

If I have a brother I shall not falter
His critical advice I shall not alter
For my mistakes and bloopers he will monitor
With his critical support I shall grow taller

Rest assured my defense is ensured
Although I'm matured
Nevertheless my steps are unsure
Unless I have my back secured

YET YOU CALL ME A BROTHER

Once I swallowed a lump of sugar
Of tea spoon measure to quench hunger
You smote me thinking it was a measure similar
To a spade full of sugar from a jar
Yet you call me a brother

You subjected me to torture authority
Turning my head upside down with sympathy never
Until I vomited out intestines
Yet you call me a brother

When you punished me with friends' cliques
You slapped them on both cheeks
As they turn one side after another so to speak
According to God's teaching techniques

As for me hither
You gave one stunning blow harder
On my forehead stronger

In contravention to teaching of GOD's father
Yet you call me a brother

UNCLE

In your figure I see my Father or Mother
In the mirror you and I are together
Birds of the same feather
Flying far to gather

You are Father and Mother incarnate
Wiping tears of fate
After opening a gate
And on the table I ate

Uncle you are a photocopy of my parents
You advise me on the current issues
Send me on errands
And protect me from getting warrants

AUNT

Mother and Father you are their shadow
How I appreciated the gift of a radio
You gave me at the meadow
When we were living in a ghetto

Once my parents were away
Leaving us on the highway
And putting your home duties away
You suddenly opened our gate way

Bringing the most precious gift
Nobody else could give
Stuff so delicious to wet lips
And with aroma of our parents' armpit

NIECE

Niece you are so nice
Because of blood ties
You made me rise
To escape too many mice

On the other time we stumbled
And we were in to tumble
We heard your feet rumble
And a solution was there humble

When my brother passed away
You embraced no sway
And you gave ineptitude no way
But you let your kindness win the day

NEPHEW

You are me in expansion
When you shrink you are me in action
And when you magnify, you are my nation
Going up in ascension

You are an oar for my boat to cross
Although a river is full of grass
And crocodiles are there to harass
You will make me pass by the grace of Christ

Son of my brother or sister
Do not stand aloof as a visitor
But double your steps faster
To stop rights being wiped away with a duster

GRAND FATHER

Without you neither parents nor I exist
Icon of love at your best
When I'm forlorn you call me for a kiss
Just to forget the taste I have missed

With dedication you brought up my parents
And to my foes you are a deterrent
Turning deadly hurricane
Into a sea with normal current

You custodian of family wisdom
In your small family Kingdom
I acquired roots of your richly customs
And feel secured as our ties blossoms

DR. BELLARIO AHOY NGONG GENG

GRAND MOTHER

Those days were sweet
When I used to be dirty with sweat
With open arms your welcome awaited
Preparing provisions to meet my needs

Mother of my father or mother
You are a great teacher my memory could gather
For culture and wisdom you are the author
And for the family pain and vicissitudes, you are the soother

Bastion of love and security
We look at you with curiosity
For the way you kept our unity
With such a pure peculiarity

GRANDSON

You little mirror of me
And grand ma
You are the future to be
When our eyes will no longer see

I'm a subject of envy
When they see me happy
Enjoying the charms of your company
Away they turn with their hearts heavy

Son of my daughter or son
The time we are gone

Carry our culture and traditions to the moon
From where your children will carry it beyond

GRAND DAUGHTER

I saw you curled on my child's lap
Placed in a napkin wrap
And wearing a blue cap
Enjoying a gentle nap

My heart leapt with joy
That there will be a day
She will descend with a ray
And keeps my worries at bay

A small shadow of me
And grand ma
She will be a grand ma to be
After she orders our culture to gear

DYNAMICS OF RICHES

Riches provide security and power
As it carries the owner to the tower
Where he will over look anything lower
And reveres anything above and over

When on rise the person changes all his belongings
To acquire value with higher longings
When on fall he changes all his glowing assets
To settle on lower holdings

Do not let your fortune slip out
As you hold it firm by your boot
Avoid being rude
As others are ready to loot

THIS IS A QUEER WORLD

When you are qualified
They give a job to unqualified
You get citizen application nullified
While that of a stranger solidified

Right person does not get a right place
As they play nothing else but malice
This queer person must be jealous
To deny a job to a person so bless

When rights are withheld
Justice is sent to hell
While equality is forced to kneel
As vice is held
Some come and get it sweet
As others like to wait
Some would like to quit
As the Creator waits to meet

To their fate they shed tears
To confirm their fears
Which they have for years
To others they live with sheers

Some enjoy this world
They regret leaving it gold
While others suffer untold
To regret getting old

Some by nature like you
When they see you they bow
Others by nature hate you
When they see you they vow

These are two sides of one coin
One side recites poem
While the other side lags behind
To meet the other at edge joints

This is a nature dictates
No explanation immediate
As the world rotates
Few will mourn the wicked

HIDING REAL INTENTIONS

Real intentions in a hook
Especially when devised by a rogue
Can be concealed by a crook
Beneath an innocent face look
Or by cracking a divertive joke

Soon after commission
Especially when carefully pursued along its direction
Real intentions can be exposed by actions

Since intentions like body waste waiting excretion
Must be discarded through actions on nature's discretion

Never hide bad intentions on outset
Behind your nice words in pretention to cheat
For you stand exposed to rain wet
As intentions must pass, I bet
Through action outlet

THE AGONY OF LONELINESS

Life without company is unnatural
Creator has made it central
For every creature plural
And anoint it natural

Government uses loneliness
To punish law breakers in earnest
Violators are imprisoned in darkness
As it is so painful like a bite of lioness

Human is a social animal
Among all mammals
Every male has a female
And live in herds how small

GRATEFULNESS

A price to whoever has done well
Given in return of his role

In achieving the goal
Which he performed at will

Leaving a feeling of worthiness to the receiver
Which he receives with pride ever
And a feeling of appreciation to the giver
Which he gives with surplus over

Do not prove me wrong
As long as the singing birds sing
And unless broken by a king
That friendship will last long

UNGRATEFULNESS (I)

A person unable to return a good done
He forgets the time gone
When he was out worn
And wanted to lick a bone

He returns good for bad
Rendering the friendship dead
To be replaced by tit for tat
Never to get support even though in a pit

Keep this advice close to your chest
And do not let others have even a gist
As you will be the one to learn this first
Ungratefulness is a behavior of a beast

UNGRATEFULNESS (II)

Look! Far there and see that fellow coming
Strange gait! Isn't it? See how he is walking
Holding his head up! His feet stumbling not caring
Every where his eyes are devouring
Sometimes tiptoeing
And sometimes bombarding
The ground with heavy steps not ceasing

They call him Mr. Ungratefulness
Because for a service rendered to him with kindness
Even if it is a life saving service to the best
He does not utter even a word of thanks to the nameless
Leave alone material return from his chess
To him, serving him is his birth right just like mother breast
God Bless

For him to say thank you even to a deity
Lends a disgrace to his outstanding dignity
But whenever it happens to offer you small for pity
He would expect you to openly recognize it with much publicity
And spread the news all over a city
For other people to know his benevolence personality
Queer is this behavior that attracts unprecedented curiosity!

HOW TO GET WHAT YOU WANT

Here is how it is found
Be specific about the amount

Know that it is with the target bound
Define its exchange in pound

Before looking for what you want
Expecting to be given as fun
Look for what he is fond of
For he will release it on gain

Assemble all factors to agree
And kneel down to ponder a pray
Allow luck to try
While knowing that nothing is got free

COWARDICE AND BRAVERY

Cowardice is there when the safety margin is wide
No matter whether there is a might
Bravery occurs when the safety margin is tight
No matter how dangerous a fight

A coward loses when there was chance to win
Because he hides himself in the dustbin
A brave person loses when he has worn his power thin
His last weapon is a pin

Do not make the safety margin too wide
And not too tight
How exactly the right guide
Depends on a reason to fight

LIAR AND TRUTH TELLER

A liar says what is far from the truth
To truth he has no trust
A truth teller says what is near from the truth
To truth he finds growth

Who does not trust truth loses credibility
Because he suffers from disability
A truth teller has credibility
Because he does not suffer irritability

Lying is good when it does not harm
Sometimes it can give an alarm
Truth telling is bad when it harms
For that reason it is damned

GOOD AND BAD PERSON

A good person is the one who gives
A portion of his harvest of olives
To other people to reap
He would want others to live
Even though it causes his pocket to weep

A bad person is the one who takes
A portion of other peoples cakes
Using tactics shrewd and fake
He never minds about their empty bags
And poverty swallowing them to their necks

The strange part in this scenario
Is that the bad person armed with arrows
Considers himself a hero
Never does he wink his eyes brows
To know that he does not par though
With a rubbish thrown out of window

FLATTERER

On his art to please a boss
He cracks jokes
Turns lies into toasts
As a victim licks his nose

The target is mesmerized
In other aspect tantalized
Facts do not arise
As they do not have price

Flatterers get away with what they want
Swinging their waists around as they hunt
The target remains with wounds
And a purse full of sand

FRIENDSHIP

Tie between people
Those who want to live jovial
They like the color purple
And desire to eat apples

Mutual interest is the bond
This holds them to each other so fond
One thing can render friendship none
Divergent interests can make it gone

Common interest gives them common tune
Lack of it leads to ruin
It destroys all life beyond imagination
Leaving instead sand dunes

ESCAPE FROM LEOPARD CLAWS

I was at the river to quench my thirst
It was so intense to resist
Not knowing that I had put myself at risk
To my surprise the leopard was the first

Although I was at downstream
She complained I made water dirty cream
I reminded her of her position upstream
Still adamant she wanted to make my life a dream

At a split of a second
I was already gone
To the bosom I'm fond
Of which I have a bond

HATRED

When you long for something
Which you are seeing
But not possessing
The interest is there ringing

When opposed interests clash hatred is born
Very soon it grows horns
Goring the unity torn
As the body goes down the drain

Hatred can be controlled
When a win/win goal is central
And wisdom having a role
To set a stage to a full

DIALOGUE BETWEEN WELL TO DO AND LESS TO DO (ERSTWHILE FRIENDS)

"Why always knock my door?
What are you looking for?
Your visit makes me bore
If you press I will roar"

"But we were best friends before
Have you forgotten the hour?
When we were together poor
And we had to search bins for food"

"To that relationship I tore
And do not remind me of days soar
If you continue to complain more
Next time you will knock a door of war"

INSPECTORS' TIP

Do you want to know in precision?
The efficiency of an institution
In order to plan a vision
With a help of a tuition
To achieve a mission

At the door step
Let your eyes rove
When boss is work gripped
And staff with thin wage
And burning in rage

See that the institution you know
Is performing low
Only a short time before they bow
To a wishful and nervous foe
That is welcoming them to his jaw

FROM FRYING PAN TO FIRE

One time I was rearing cattle
I heard bullets as they rattle
It was an advancing battle
I thought to hide like a turtle

So that I can drive cattle away
But alas! They were already on my way
I ran towards the leeway
Hiding under the bridge bay

A cobra was lying under the bridge bed
I set on its middle, I bet
The beast surrounded me mad
Its twitches sent me almost dead

ON BEING A MAVERICK

Maverick, Maverick you are free
Happy, happy to a degree
How much I envy thee
I wish we meet to agree

Be where democracy is rooted
And has your back patted
If not lavishly honored
As your opinion suited

Never be where you may be persecuted
If you fail to be executed
You will be hated
If not looted

DR. BELLARIO AHOY NGONG GENG

THE WHEEL OF JUSTICE TURNS SLOW

Do not run fast
Go slowly like an ass
To reach the court last
Justice has eyes down cast

Even if your rights glow
Exposing your opponent hollow
And be on the side of law
The wheel of justice turns slow

Even if you bellow
Heat iron red yellow
And let the tears flow
The wheel of justice turns slow

RUMOUR IS TALL AND RUNS FASTER

A friend of a rumor wondered
What makes you hurried?
And neatly ordered
Tall and run faster

As I'm tall I look into the future
Guess people expectations faster
And deliver my message at leisure
There it runs faster, like Saturn yonder

Like a thief, I attack my target quicker
And get my trophy secured

Before I disappear faster
That is the secret of my nature

TRUTH IS SMALL, THIN AND HANDSOME

A young lady decried as she stood
Society is so crude
Basic fabric is left to rot
And unable to offer good
Let us look for something shrewd

An old man responded quicker
Truth, truth is the answer
He is keen to remember
When rights are trodden over
To bring injustice closer

But truth beautiful as a pearl
Is as small as a cereal
Thin as an aerial
And tends to wander like a squirrel

LIE IS TALL, FAST AND UGLY

She saw a figure towering a crowd
All others measure to his throat
A young man of a complexion coffee-shroud
She thought that would make her proud

On a final whistle he was ahead faster
Clearly on a running race he is a master
His colleagues call him bastard
For a race craft he has mustered

When she met the man close, things fell apart
He has a head that of a bird
And a monkey face that looks like a heart
Her heart sunk, allowing tears to depart

WHEN TIME TICKS TOO SLOW

When time ticks too slow
Never allow the blame to flow
Neither against the solar law
Nor to the watch device below

Either blame great urge to satisfy ego
For its desire to skip the door but the window
Or decry a constricting row
That has been there for some time ago

Bear nothing but patience
For natural laws are inflexible in essence
Furthermore this was a fashion
Being practiced so much by ancients

WHEN TIME IS TICKING TOO FAST

Congratulations for your time crest
Why should you be in haste?
After your dice has been cast
Your fortunes are vast

Just relax and frequently hold toasts
Forget the unhappy past
When problems were to your chest
And you had to take poverty your guest

Although your friends agree with you
Nature will not bow
And stop the time go
For you to slowly row

CRITICISM

Criticism hurts
Its chatters ego to parts
It can also blow out dirt
From the floor soiled by birds

Criticism is a blessing
When it carries out cleansing
It can also be a cursing
When it causes heads clashing

Be careful when making criticism
For it can either drop you happily

Into a sea of wisdom
Wherein resides freedom
Or can make you fall into a dungeon
Inhabited by sadism

HOME IS HOME

Even if you stay in Rome
And live a life full of pomp
With your sweet heart Tom
Home is home

Although you hold a million Euros
And a house adorned with roses
Being hailed a hero among heroes
Home is home though with cons and pros

Though home stinks of dead mouse
And you have to pause
To catch your nose
Home is home even if infested by louse

MY PEOPLE

When I was abandoned and deported
I was hopeless and depleted
But you had me comforted
With every support you afforded

How I love you my people
As a gift I will send you an apple
To fall and makes water ripple
That will cover a swimming couple

As I live, I'm for you
For your boat, I shall row
To the distance your eyes saw
To the land you will till and sow

REACTIONS OF PEOPLE TO INSULTS

When insults come from powerful person
They are considered advice from saint
Efforts are made to calm the situation down
And contents are given sweet version

When insults come from equals
Relations make way to tensions
The situation may need a surgeon
To diffuse it with some exertion

But when insults come from a weak person
They are considered unsolicited aggression
That must be met exacting retribution
All condemn a person to cardinal sin

MORAL NATURE OF PEOPLE

Either all people are good but forced to be bad
By conditions that drive them mad
They can do what?
If the powerful are ready to have their throat cut
And deprive them from what they produce to eat

Or essentially they are bad but pretend to be good
This they do to prevent being booed
Under cover of good they hide being rude
To tread unaware with a boot
In order to take a loot

Or they are half bad and half good
Depending on what is in the wood
If it is a lion they turn odd
And if it is a gazelle they shoot
For very soon they will enjoy the food

PARADOXES OF LIFE (I)

A Thief wants to steal
But he does not want at all
His properties to be stolen even a little
He considers protecting them vital
To extent of sending a culprit to jail

A prostitute engages in prostitution
But she does not encourage a notion
Of her daughter to be in a sex auction

Or her conducting a training tuition
Making sex job as her life contribution

A ruler wants to rule for life
Preferring his offspring to continue to drive
But does not want others to dive
In power imitating his type
He would swear to chop that plan with a knife

PARADOXES OF LIFE (II)

One fights for a cause zealously
And makes a U turn to ruin it costly
The reasons are personal mostly
But use a public cause to justify it completely

One condemns corruption bid
When others are doing it
But condones it indeed
When he or relatives opens its lid

One fights tougher
In order to bring democracy over
But when in power
He brings it down lower

PARADOXES OF LIFE (III)

Whatever good utterances for public sake
A shrewd leader makes

And whatever plans he undertakes
Attempting to divide the public cake

The plans are pulled down
By the self interest clowns
Because a leader is a victim marooned
By a personal interests of clones

The individual interest haunts him for days
In everything he does and in everything he says
At the end he surrenders to self interest pages
Leaving fans waving good bye

PARADOXES OF LIFE (IV)

A bad person is that one who renders people dead
But when he kills for a good cause he is praised flat
Indicating that there is no absolute good and absolute bad
Both good and bad are relative in their fate

A good person is that who saves livelihoods
But if he saves a life of a criminal brute
He is criminal en route
Indicating that not every life saving exercise is good

A good person gives gifts to people for help
But if he gives thieves in order to lay a crime valve
He is a thief himself
Indicating that not every giving of gifts is good for itself

PEOPLE AND WHAT THEY DO

On one hand People always remember the good things they have done
At least they long for others to offer appreciation
If they cannot pay them back soon
At the worst scenario they want favor back before noon

On the other People never know the bad things they have done in totality
They are always at odds with those who remind them pretty
At least they want people to apologize to them as penalty
If not it can lead to long standing enmity

In all People need to be praised even if they do not deserve good
It is so practiced a habit that it has become a disciplinary code
They call it diplomatic clout
Those who do not practice it are like people in the nude

RESOURCES AND PEOPLE'S RELATIONS

When resources are in abundance
Relations flourish among people
People talk of common nipple
And nationalism flares like water ripple

When resources are relatively meager
Selfishness dominates and relations sink deeper
Hypocrisy reigns extensive and stronger
And nationalism grows weaker

When resources are too meager and famine in full
Relations are severed even among related souls
Robbery takes place as nationalism dies cool
Survival of the fittest is the rule

PANACEA TO ALL WORLD'S PROBLEMS *(A Reminder)*

If people do to others
What they accept to be done to them hither
People will never commit mistakes thither
And the world will enjoy lasting peace ever

Never jump to your feet Oh people!
Surprised by this statement simple
But try individually three folds
At your family and friends level

The results are at the gratifying rate
In refreshing and cementing relation states
This is not human made for trade
As Holy Scriptures bear witness up to date

IN PEACE WITH MYSELF

When I spent time alone
Thinking of what can be sown
And spend less time on my own
Thinking of what is in the moon

When I do useful things at will
That I can do diligently with skill
And with satisfactory outcome zeal
That brings revenue and income to fill

When I avoid doing things that dwarf
My reputation and Health valve
And do things that help by unit times twelve
Then I'm at peace with my self

IN PEACE WITH OTHERS

When I do to others just
What I like others to put in my nest
Without me complaining of its taste
Or murmuring at least

When I share with others their sorrow
For their unfortunate situation I know
And help them morally and materially at ago
As my means could allow
When injustice gathers
And rights of others suffer
And I am there to put right their case matter
I shall be in peace with others

BRIDE

They call me bride
Not because I'm intelligently bright

But because I'm going to be tied
To a person of my pride

I look forward for a happy journey
Being accompanied by sweet honey
Alone we ride a beautiful pony
At its back our lips join in a moment so lovely

What next does one want in this world?
If one has a husband from gold
When however you fall
Will keep you on hold

BRIDE GROOM

They call me bridegroom
Because I groom the bride room
I must take care to prevent her nightmares
As this will bring to our home doom

As time passes driven by nature
I do not wait for her paws to mature
Lest they will inflict our love immature
For potentials are there promising sure

I must decide to play deaf in line
Of not to hear any report maligned
And request her to play blind
Not to see my uncalled for smile with a client

THE YOUNG GENERATION (I)

Look! What daddy is doing below the hill?
Why is he digging the field?
Why has he always to deal?
With a cow dung filth
Why does mum always kneel?
To sweep the compound with delight and zeal

You see John my friend
I also could not understand
Why they take that trend
Using their hands
To disturb the land
They may be doing it for fun

When I inquire they say with frown
That they are getting food from the ground
And milk from cows raised and kept around
Mum also says she sweeps the compound
To throw the garbage in the pit
To keep the rage of diseases down

THE YOUNG GENERATION (II)

I see ee! But you see friend, all facts collected
These older generations have stagnated
Moving backward and outdated
With computer, all is programmed and animated
They can strike an icon for farm processing already formulated
And get food within few minutes while seated

The same thing with milk John
Whereby computer cows you own
Can give you milk in a second
I do not even mention
The sweeping of a ground
This can happen before a second has gone

Come out in big numbers Oh! Dot com. generation
Come out and shun the physical work of older population
And embrace the development done in a split of time motion
Down! Down! With the slow thinking brains of chameleons
Very soon we shall explore with intense determination
The galaxies and establish colonies beyond imagination!

HUMAN BEHAVIOR AND WEALTH

From outer space without stop
A giant telescope fitted with microscope
From a super being
Beamed into our globe
With an aim to probe
The human behavior visa-a-vise wealth scope
The results are startling hiccups

When people are half way close
No poor and no rich
They are human up to their toes
Helping others under their noses
And advancing human cause
They respect each other without pause
And fear God laws

When some are rich
They turn giant turtles under a bridge
They sleep on their fellow human as they wish
And make them victims under siege
They press them down
And suck their body juices like leeches
Rendering them necked and exposed on beeches

When many are poor
They also turn beasts
Inform of wolves and boars
They break doors
And become robbers up to the core
The insecurity caused as in war
Can invite anarchy to prevail

HUMAN BEHAVIOR ANALYSED (I)

Sir, wait for me sir
How can you explain dear?
These four scenarios here
That lay bare human nature there
Understanding them clear
Is mind boggling, unable to bear
For a long time I'm in split hairs
Looking for someone knowledgeable to share

What is it my child about?
How can I help you, I doubt?
I'm rushing to a meeting closed in a shroud
Where stakes are being portioned out

If I'm far like clouds
No one cares to give a mouth
With my presence, they will give me before I shout
To impress that they are good above the crowd

Ah! Oh yes
But that is the topic I want to raise
Of human nature there are four scenarios now days
Which one fits its normal situation?
In one scenario one is self centered as for others he never gives a grace
In second scenario one is good to self as for others he is also nice
In the third scenario one is uncaring to self and never have relationship ties
In the fourth scenario one condemns self and for others he showers praises

HUMAN BEHAVIOR ANALYSED (II)

That is by far simple
And obvious my child
The one who is self centered in all
And never gives a grace to others is in all spell
The normal nature
Human share this role
With other animals
Look around and prove before you yield

But since human is a social animal so placed
Doing this openly will expose him to deface

To hate and isolation
He covers this up to the waist
By engaging in a second scenario
That is doing well to self in utter grace
And pretending to be nice
While underneath the real intent lies

He reverts back never minded
To the first scenario
As soon as people take him for granted
This second scenario is the one adopted
By societies as their conduct code
Human common institutions
Including governments
Are made on the bases of actions pretended

As for the third scenario, it is for lunatics
Because a normal person, even a fanatic
Cannot self inflict and live in isolation

The fourth scenario is the behavior characteristic
Of a mentally retarded classic
As normal person cannot be self drastic
And to others showers praises as tactics

HUMAN BEHAVIOR ANALYSED (III)

I see ee!
It now grows in me
But prophets all agree
That doing bad is a key

Work of a Satan in his plea
To woo away people so free
From under God's blessed tree
In its work of removing comfort and glee

There is no contradiction
With this principle in connection
Satan has been in friction
With human nation
Since creation
So much so that fraction by fraction
It has inculcated through accumulation
This character to human natural configuration

To change this natural pattern
God has to start with changing the Satan
And since doing bad in return
Is the very nature of Satan
The struggle will be so great in heaven
So fierce, long and blatant
That the impact may come staggering in a garden
After Human epoch had been already forgotten

WOLVES IN SHEEP CLOTHES

Grand Pa hallo
I'm greatly disturbed thorough
By this problem that makes emotions flow
In life who makes it to flourish and glow?
Is it the fellow?
Who does good things away from the shadow?

Or the one who walks the street narrow
And does bad things without blinking the eye brow?

Why grandchild let us go home
The answer is obvious and prompt
It is a person well groomed
Who does good things
That progresses well in life without shame
Good things are blessed by God in the womb
To religious communities they are welcome
And smiled upon by your ancestors in their tombs

But grand Pa dear
There is a problem here
I have seen people doing good things fair
And sometimes end up miserably there
And I saw people doing bad things without fear
But they are living happily with their peers
I want to enjoy my life without tear
Whom should I emulate and share?

You are right grandchild you argue like a rebel
Those who do good things are like angels
But they do encounter problems on their table
Explained by religious preachers in the bible
As temptations from the devil
They urge people to overcome every evil
Sometimes they do succeed feeble
Before they are called to heaven

As for those brute
Who do bad things in the wood?

And they succeed in life hood
They do them weighing odds
Under pretentions of being good
They are wolves in sheep suits
Do you want to be one of them my blood?
I do not advise you to do so under my watch

RELATIONS ARE FUNCTION OF INTERESTS

Why do you cry foul you idiot?
You better learn in a statute
That relation is fitting like suit
When interests converge among patriots
Why are you so nostalgic about that period?
About your past relationship
Now broken and in ruin

Now know this fact and strive to teach
In the past they existed with high pitch
Because you were eating in one dish
As some of them become powerful and rich
Interests are not any longer at reach
If you want back your relations as you wish
Heed this advice to curb out a niche

Either you become rich a monster
Or powerful usurper
Or you wait longer
Until you meet in eternal life proper
Where interests purified by the Giver
Will be the same again on the alter
Under the watchful eyes of the Equalizer

IF THIEVES ARE GETTING FAT THE VICTIMS MUST BE GETTING THIN

Look my Angel!
One does not need to see with an eye of an eagle
Or superhuman mind to comprehend in detail
Some people who were as small as beetles
Are becoming fatter and fatter the size of a jungle
In terms of properties they own while they are idle

While others become thinner
And this takes place faster
In span of time shorter
Does it mean they work harder?
And faster than others
What is happening there?

My friend sincerely,
There are two ways of getting rich quickly
By robbing people violently
And by stealing people's properties secretly
All of them are thieves definitely
Because they take what they do not own legally

I need not belabor this point after my boss
Because as simple calculations goes
When one gains the other must lose
And so if you see some people getting fat without any cause
And others getting thin up to their toes
Then thieves must be among them wearing sheep blouses

IMPORTANCE OF EDUCATION (I)

Education! God curses your praises
Why waste money on nonsense
On something you can do without wastes
Look around and see all these riches
I did not need education for answers
But through physical prowess
With tactics and intrigues as spices

No, Mr. powerful sir,
Even if you acquire wealth elsewhere
Still education is important and useful my dear
It will enable you keep your wealth with care
And helps giving you a holistic view of far and near
Conducting your behavior to humane gear
And never veer to the beast style of life

Come on my champion!
You my critical Advisor in action
Come closer and lend me your ears with attention
I tell you this and let others not know without my permission
You think I'm a fool without any direction?
I know the importance and usefulness of education
But what shall I gain if now I give recognition?

IMPORTANCE OF EDUCATION (II)

The Educated will damn me
Into a dust bin
And roll me over down a valley

I must be in this position I have been
By hooks and crooks to their chagrin
Meanwhile I educate my children
To take over down the road

Oh! I recollect before getting far
Your children will serve in my children store
Even if they are educated hordes
And your wife will handle my household chores
When my wife is away to the shore
And you will be my critical Advisor
Have we an accord to adore?

Yes, Mr. powerful, yes
What can I say to you guys?
If power has let the truth dies
And lies are made to rise
Whatever they say is wise
He said these wiping tears
From his eyes thrice

NO THEY ARE NOT MAD THEY ARE FOOLS

Once one person has a chance to be rich
Because he had power to unleash
Using it, he acquired a niche
But for fear of integrity breach
He gave money to a custodian to clinch
Without legal arrangement stitched
When he lost influence after power switch
The custodian took money under siege
Denied the owner and rendered him a son of a bitch

DR. BELLARIO AHOY NGONG GENG

Then the other person went up a hill
Sending his relatives to hell
And gave genuine guardians nil
As he brought his opponents to fill
And taking care of a shield
In a gesture to capture their will
At the end they turn against him
And had him drink a bitter pill
Before his fate was sealed

Another again wielded a big club
To fight a lion caught in a trap
The lion exhausted with slaps
Fainted dead on the ground steps
The man removed a net just enough
For the lion to spring back prompt
Lodging its claws and stab
A man dead and devoured him
Leaving traces of meat and bones as they dropped

Why do they play in a dangerous pool?
Are they mad like a wounded mule?
No they are not mad at all
They are fools
Because a mad person as we are told
Can get treatment tools
Either within the hospital aisle
Or among religious schools
But a fool has no cure as a rule

PASSING THROUGH A HOLE OF A NEEDLE (I)
(A dialogue between desperate Young people and an Elder)

Young people:
"Dear elder, what we own
Are taken by an enemy at dawn
They attack us with guns
And when we run away with pants
They loot and burn our houses to soot

Without guns we are in danger
And we hear further
That if we cross a border
To the east we get an answer
From enemies of our enemies proper

But we are afraid going there
As it is very far
And there are a lot, Oh dear!
Of obstacles on the way to detour
For your advice, we long for, for you care"

Elder:
"You are between two dangers
If you do not go, you youngsters
You will either die by the enemy killers
Or die by disease and hunger
As there is nothing to support survivors

Better die looking for power
Than perish trying to cower
You better go east a tower

Than to remain here a bower
Where you will meet a mower

Your great parents' souls
Dwelling against the GOD's wall
Will guide you reach your goal
And allow you pass small
Through a needle hole"

PASSING THROUGH A HOLE OF A NEEDLE (II) (ADVICE OF AN ELDER)
(A dialogue between desperate Young people and an Elder)

Young people:
"We know that with us are great parents
Reality is that our wealth including current
Are taken away by force from orient
While spirits of elders were impotent
And watching helplessly without deterrent

Also you elder is telling us all
To pass through a needle hole
This is more absurd a goal
As we do not see the possibility at all
Of us passing through a hole too small

This is chasing a wind by a mob
You better tell us to surrender to a hanging rope
Than to give us false hope
That could not be achieved prompt
Even with prayers of Pope"

Elder:
"I see you are desperately deprived
But if you do good things that preserve life
And avoid bad things that destroy its type
Except on self defense drive
That is passing through a hole with delight

Your ancestors in the past tried all these
Those loyal to rules succeeded with ease
Battering their cheeks with kisses
While those who faltered regretted
Filling air with pleas

Nature is both compassionate and brute a lot
Depending whether you follow her rule or not
Followers are hailed with victory vote
While defaulters are damned in a dungeon throat
Those who have ears hear this advice, you will never regret

PRIVATE INTEREST VERSUS PUBLIC INTEREST

Private interest has always differed
And continues to fight public interest
They are expected to compromise but never
The fight continues from now and for ever
Until life ceases to exist hither

Private interest insists that it cares
Since it is the one in charge so far
It must take the lion share
But Lo! In what quantity and for how long it dares?
Since its satisfaction has no limit declared

Public interest says is the multiple of the private
And the one who produces and creates
Everything must pass its gate
Otherwise the private loses trade
As the war rages and so the debate

SELFISHNESS IS THE ROOT CAUSE OF ALL WOES

Selfishness promotes self interest
It kills rights of others fast
As for its owner, it feasts
Blinds the owner and places him on deaf list
Thus promoting corruption at best

Public interest preserves rights for each
Including that of a selfish
It is ever hearing, ever seeing and rich
In dispensing fairness and justice as you wish
Please consult his Advisor, Discipline as you reach

Selfishness is the root cause of all woes
It is the cause of divisions and countless wars
It can be tamed by laws
But keeps popping out its nose
From the cage as time goes

THE SOURCE OF A FATAL BLOW

I stood in awe to look at this situation compared to none
For any person there are friends and enemies

The number and strength of each group
Depend on a status of a person
The stronger a person, the more of friends and enemies won

There are two types of friends
One group is committed and has sincerity of parents
They are too few to run an errand
The other group has an opportunistic trend
They are as many as the population of orients

When one is in trouble milieu
Only a handful of friends stand by elbow
While opportunistic friends stand by the meadow
And become source of a fatal blow
To cover up, they allow crocodile tears to flow

The real enemies do not strike a fatal crash
Because they are far and under close watch
Any of their movement is easily fetched
And its elements are caught as they rush
Being betrayed by the opportunistic batch

WHEN YOUR CALLS ARE RECEIVED WITH JOY

When your calls are received with joy
You must be controlling resources tray
Either you are rich, powerful or influential guy
To affect a receiver in a fundamental way
Along the direction of his interest lay

Your voice wears a golden ring
And your statements carry glad tidings
Which are recorded by brain link
They can be retained in memory store
Without writing them down

Ceremony mood prevails and glowing
Soon after you stop your calling
As this changes a status bearing
And changing status rating
In an upward direction is a blessing

WHEN YOUR CALLS ARE RECEIVED WITH RELUCTANCE

When your calls are received with reluctance
You must be an empty lot with nothing to lend
With no power and no riches as net balance
From dish to mouth you live by chance

Your voice sounds coarse and brittle
Your talk is bothersome a little
And has no match for their title
For whatever you say is offensive in total

Mood of regrets follow your call blares
No such calls will be received in future days
You can try to recall using sound snares
But will not be long before they fall on deaf ears

OLD AND YOUNG PERSONS

Old and young persons are jacks of one trade
If you teach an old person a machine to operate
He would prepare to narrate
And if you make the young person to create
He would prepare to modulate

One person is skilful
With a mind cool
And the other is resentful
Desiring to use a tool
Each side wants to force a pull

Otherwise they can complement each other
If they chose to work together
The older group can apply their skill as advisers
While young group can implement plans as bulldozers
Because all of them are birds wearing the same feathers

EFFECT OF BLIND SUPPORT

To a leader of doubtful capacity
There is a great possibility
Of leading supporters to calamity
For no one will dare speaking reality
As he may be branded guilty
For retracting his loyalty

To a supporter, a great possibility is afoot
Of committing mass suicide with speed

For when a leader stumbles a bit
They stumble too on it
And when he falls in a pit
They will follow suit

Wise is a leader on board
Who does not accept blind support
But instead accept critical recourse
To constructive support blessed by God
For with it mutual interest lays on the road
And is born robust and kicking like a toad

I KNOW YOU

Even though you slow your pace
Blank your gaze
And hide your face
In order to appear nice
I know you and you do not know me

Even if you pretend to be innocent
And distribute smiles as you want
Avoid your house and live on a rent
And shed crocodile tears to cover an event
I know you and you do not know me

Even if you appear religious
Ardently pious
Articulating statements that amuse
With verses from Bible good news
I know you and you do not know me

Even though you strain a smile
That continues for a while
With intention of deceiving a poor girl
Standing away for a tenth of a mile
I know you and you do not know me

Even though you dramatize my welcome
And send me on mission with Tom
In order to forget the wound
You inflicted on me
I know you and you do not know me

Even though you play innocence
And shed tears as you land
To mesmerize those sent
For the funeral of Ann
I know you and you do not know me

WHO IS A GOOD FRIEND?

The one who sticks
To relationship when you are sick
No matter how you are weak
Is there to kiss your cheek

The one who sticks on
To relationship when you are imprisoned
Serving the sentence alone
In an area isolated from free zone

The one who sticks fast
To relationship when you are powerless
And sinking deep in problems up to waist
But preventing them from reaching your chest

WHO IS A FAKE FRIEND?

The one who poises friendly
When you are healthy
Share to avoid with you anything filthy
And admire together any one wealthy

The one who washes your dishes
When you are in riches
Ready to reduce your enemies to ashes
And suck your wealth like leeches

The one who eagerly pull
Relationship when you are powerful
But when to the brim full
Will leave you regretful

FINDING A GOOD WIFE OR HUSBAND TO BE

If you want to find through a direct approach you miss
Because every person hides negative side at best
After commitment they unleash it causing a fall on knees
Only rare luck can put your shattered life together at peace

The best is through companion approach frame
If companion behaviors meet your dream
You are nearer to your desire flame
Do not hesitate to fill your love to a glass brim

If companion behaviors are not attractive to you
Because they love styles stranger than what you know
You better withdraw earlier before you make a vow
To avoid being pierced by a lifelong arrow

MY AGE MATES

You are a yardstick
Against which I measure strict
My progress stocks
As life ticks

As a teacher you stand tall on a hill
Because you gave me life skills
That molded my life real
And strengthen my power will

You are a wall I lean to
When I'm being pursued by a foe
For without you
My days are counted down a loo

DR. BELLARIO AHOY NGONG GENG

THE DAY I FELT LONELY

The day I felt lonely, robbed of joy
Was that fateful day
When news loaded with dismay
Declared that my mother passed away

My accounts were on credit
Relatives were far to meet
And my only friend was on permit
Everything seemed decayed except my wit

On that day darkness reigned
I washed with awe as it landed
It was not a one sided band
But was closing in from up and down

VALUE OF A DIALOGUE

Folks of my country, wake! It is 6 o'clock
Exercise the value of a dialogue
To overcome problems under lock
To move forward, you are blocked

Dialogue is both effective and cheap
It can prevent millions to weep
And enable billions to reap
Allowing peace to creep

Embrace dialogue by tooth and nail
Even if the first round fails
For when people stop to smile
Guns will begin to wail

OBITUARY POEM

Lual Lual Akuei of South Sudan Clan
How great you are!
As a son you made your father proud
By letting his head tower among the crowd
As a father you laid a foundation for a nation on the ground
And as a husband you shared indivisible love without frown
As a leader you knew the future of your flock around
Lual Lual Akuei of South Sudan Clan
How stoic you are!
Your life was destined to stay as engraved
But a notorious ailment cut short your life craving
It caught your hand and forced you to wave
But you caught its neck and taught it to behave
Until both of you are laid in the same grave
Lual Lual Akuei of South Sudan Clan
How victorious you are!
The disease thought it was in a position to dictate
But you were victorious instead
Because you went to join your ancestors great
Sitting beside the throne of GOD straight
As for disease, it neither has ancestors nor GOD to accept its parade

NATURE, WHY TAKE AWAY MY BROTHER?
(Attribute to late General Santo Ayang Deng)

Nature you gave me a brother
I was so happy to have him nearer
To be my brother and a playmate proper
For anything I need he has an answer

Suddenly you removed him from our home
And thrust him at your bosom
From thence I'm left lonely like a tomb
With no one to call and echo my name

I have succumbed to you Oh Mother Nature!
Since this is your choice pure
From now I shall not again count his number
His fate and mine are under your care

RECEPTION OF TRAGEDY AT TIARALIET

It was Thursday 16/02/2012 at 3.00 PM
The ambulance siren vibrated like a dream
Sounding the arrival of a body of a prime
A young man crushed by a truck in a crime

The whole town rushed to the scene in uproar
To follow the body to the burying core
The site was full of people and were increasing more
To witness the lowering of the body to the resting floor

The man was so courageous, industrious and young
Community singer who became popular not so long
Father did not attend the burial as he had no bones or tongue
The young man name was Gel Koor Malong

WITH HUMAN NATURE, ANY TREATMENT YOU WILL GET

With human nature you can tell
Any treatment can sell
For humane treatment to yield
There are people who will offer it well
To the level you love the human beings big and small

And for horrible treatment unleashed
There are those who can make it accomplished
To the level of thinking foolish
All human kind is devilish
And that life is hellish

The reason is that people
By human nature are placed noble
Astride good and evil
Borrowing a seep from either level
Without any trouble

BRIDE THROWN OUT OF WINDOW

He did not want to marry at all
Because he had married to alcohol

But people of his kin and kith in whole
Wanted him to marry a girl
Beautiful and tall
To meet their inheritance goal

After much pull and push
He succumbed like a bush
Under the fire deluge
Alcohol he ceased to touch
And bore the marriage torch
Although his face was bruised
When they were alone with bride Rose
He broke the alcohol pause
One night after having a heavy dose
He slept on the marital bed in the house
With clothes and shoes on his body loose
He was unable to put his brain to use

The bride came to assist him with delight
By removing the clothes first alright
And when she touched shoes slight
He got up with stupor and kicked the bride
He mindlessly opened the window right
Seized her and threw her out straight!

ROOTS OF A PERSON

A person has many roots for care
In order to anchor with for years
The same way trees
Anchored themselves so far

With multiple roots layers
They exist in six pairs

A pair for mother and father
A pair for brother and sister
Pair for maternal and paternal uncles
A pair for maternal and paternal Aunts
A pair for friends at the corner
A pair for son and daughter

If all roots are healthy, active and good
You are the strongest person ever stood
If all roots are dead then you are dead in the wood
The good news is that considering all odds
One can survive among brutes
Even with one healthy and active root

THE DISTRESS CAUSED BY RECKLESS CHILDREN

When children disregard parental advice
And succumb to their vices
That has no hope as time advances
The distress creeps in like a water tide on rise
To heighten parental crises

Worry and loss of hope as they stood
Command the mood
Parental hearts are laden with soot
As they cannot bear the behavior so rude
And cannot fathom their lifestyles so crude

Step up home education if you can
For not to have children is not a gain
But life littered with pain
Just like losing them as strays is in the main
Rendering you a prisoner in chain

MARITAL RELATIONS

Marriage is an institution sanctioned by nature
And made it pure
Nothing can be better and sure
Even if you render cancer cure

Before marriage the couples to be know half of each other
Because each shows their negative side not
In an attempt to woo the other side along
After marriage they cannot hide any longer

For marriage, hurry not
Give yourself time to note
It is when you wait and weigh a lot
Can a happy marriage be got

TREASON

He was imprisoned in a dungeon
As dark as a cloudy night in June
Tight to poles with ropes of iron
Neck constricted with a yoke of a devil creation
Starved with no food saved soup of onion

He stood upright, his wails never attracted attention
His face down cast as if battered by sand dunes
He longs for a rescue beyond

I came with that rescue, no joke
Armed with all weapons in vogue
But most important of all I took
Was determination of a hunting dog
For no way can a suffering look
Of my kind continue unabated under my wake
I cut the ropes and removed the yoke
And drag him out for sun bath like a frog

Not long before setting of the dawn
He forgot of his suffering moments
Colluded with his former enemy band
To have my finger cut off with a knife of his gun!
I pleaded for his help as before he had done
But turned away his face as if stroke by a mighty hand
Leaving me in tears, anguish and forlorn
What a person is he? Is he human?

WHEN FORMER ENEMIES BECOME FRIENDS

When former enemies are in friendship
Two speculations come around
Either they are deceiving themselves
One taking the other for a ride

Or they have struck a new mutual deal
Having abundance yield

To support their livelihood
Or having a common enemy at their heels

Stay alert and be watchful double
If hyenas and dogs with enmity terrible
Are in friendship bond
Human beings must be in trouble

PUBLIC SERVICE VERSUS PRIVATE SERVICE

Those supposed to render public services
In actual fact do engage in private affairs
Since they have access to public resources
To finance their own including some for nieces
They pray for God to prolong their days

While those engaged in private business
Do actually run public services dictates
Since they bear the brand of taxation plate
Needed to swell the public coffers in wait
They long for a day free from taxes rates

Is there a need of public services to kick?
The need of a public service is bleak
But a lean and not a huge one can do at the peak
Provided that it is composed of colleagues
Who have lost senses of smell, sight and appetite

Deep in debt

Deep in debt
Your dignity is dead
Your credibility once fat
Loses weight to become a thread

Regain your worth by working hard
And with a balance mind set
Instead of speculating at any rate
To fly out with a jet
Thinking that you will escape
And avoid payment

Wise are the people when they see red
They trace their feet back to toil and sweat
In order to pay their debt
Even though they are in a rut
As life worth lodges few feet
Near a deep hole full of rats

Prayers of the deceived and humiliated

Oh Creator of Earth and Heaven!
Listen to my prayers for my heart is broken
As I'm deceived and humiliated by men
This is what they have done

They told me to fight for our rights together
But when we had achieved that clearer
I was excluded from the share proper
Putting instead their relatives and friends

They told me to till
I thought it was a deal
But they took away the produce yields
Leaving me kicking my heels

Oh Creator! They urged me to study hard to top
After I have finished and bearing hope
They denied me a job
To sustain my life and cope

Now I'm left hungry and homeless
The period of waiting will be timeless
Before I succumb to a pit bottomless
I plead for you to give them this retribution painless

Do not give them the benefit of death domain
But allow them to eat and fill their lumens
Without sleep and movement
Forever and ever, Amen

WHEN TWO MIGHTY FIGHT

When two mighty fight
Opportunists fall victim
If they support one side
They may lose the other giant
And if they go to hide
Both will be out of sight

Their tactics involve supporting Jane
Without the knowledge of Ann

But when discovered red handed
By one or both women
They suffer consequences under the sun
And loses both favors at once

Happy those days when opportunists
Serve one powerful boss
And when he loses influence
They will support with kisses
The other who have taken over the list
Even though opposed to the first

TIME TO HARVEST

Silly! Do not say this and walk away in haste
Who is there to question my harvest?
Where was he when I was sowing seeds in the past?
I did toil, gnashed my teeth and sweated at best
I was almost to suffocate and permanently rest
If it was not God with its Angels blowing away dust

Leave me alone my friend it is night
Let me satisfy my appetite
And if there is a left over aside
I promise to give you right
After myself, family and my new bride
As well as when grand children unborn are satisfied

Just be patient for patience pays tidily
Believe me for I'm over fifty
If you do not get it now in this city

DR. BELLARIO AHOY NGONG GENG

You will get it meaty
When you and I are enjoying eternity
How beautiful? That life will drag on for infinity

CHAPTER III

NATURE AND ITS FEATURES

NATURE OF MEN

Men are by nature half men
As well as half women
If men were wholly men
There would be men without women

Human life would stop after first creation
Since a man alone cannot make procreation
Human mission will be on cessation
And nothing will be subject to narration

Life is progressive in variation
As there is a chance of combination
To create a new manifestation
Of perfect composition

NATURE OF WOMEN

Women are by nature wholly women
Nature has not made them the same with men's
If women's nature were the same with men's
There would be one without the other

Imagine the world with one sex
It will be like a lion in a den
Consuming all animals including humans
Leaving nothing to survive with

Watching at a distance
Life will disappear at the first instant
Making a way for Satan
To make an U-turn

DO NOT DISTURB MOTHER NATURE

Do not disturb the time roster
Of Mother Nature
In any seasonal weather
Because she is too busy a creature

In autumn she feeds a new born child
In winter she weans it by the Nile
In spring she exhibits a pregnant posture style
In summer she delivers a new born on a tile

In autumn again
She feeds a new born child at o'clock nine

Guess who is the child on shine?
It is yourself and siblings in line

THE RAPE OF JEBEL (MOUNT) KUJUR

Jebel Kujur my cave
In compassion wave
I'm torn apart by every raid of rape
Inflicted against your honor sake

In sympathy my heart jolts anguishing
And my tears freely flowing
When I see your beautiful shape changing
And your volume diminishing
As if you are from AIDS suffering

Government seems to be enjoying your ordeal
And great ancestral spirits from whose will
You took the name ran away in horror yell
Leaving you to your fate to kneel

I want to make an honest suggestion
Better I whisper this in your ears with caution
Lest your enemies eavesdrop it before action
Why don't we conjure up a love apparition?
Elope and go to my village bastion!

DR. BELLARIO AHOY NGONG GENG

NATURE OF PROBLEMS

Problems cannot be avoided altogether
As long as you live hither
Because they sleep with you thither
And wake up with you ever

They cannot be threatened with a knife
As long as you are alive
Because they are resilient enough
As a rubber tyre is when you drive

However you can shower them with insults
And disappear into a grave hole
They will not follow you there bold
Because they fear the grave vault

IN ACCORD WITH NATURE

Oh mother nature!
How vast is your pasture?
So continuous without rupture
One has to understand your feature
In order to be in accord with future

Fountain of multiple breasts
When I suck your nipple at rest
I have taken you under duress
But when on the nipple I press
In the gourd you quench my thirst

A mistress of stern rules
When I obey them I win a bull
And take a ride on a mule
But when I abuse them I'm a fool
Deserving to sink in a pool

NATURE OF LIFE

Life is a cruel game
Its essentials are hidden in a farm
One has to labor from dawn
To have it tamed
Before it renders one maimed

Life is wearisomely bitter
But can be made sweeter
If one has to be a fighter
And a mighty worker
Swinging in a dollar

Life is unpleasantly leveled
Poor is not only isolated like a rebel
But associated with evil
While rich is worshipped in a temple
His status falls short that of an Angel

RIVER

We appreciate you with praise
When you run down with grace

With a precious gift so bless
Demanding no price
Where ever you pass
To the living you are a host
And to the non living you are a guest
Providing terrain with what to boast

You are a natural treasure
Enjoyed by any creature
Even though a source of conflict raiser
A location without you has no measure

RAIN

Lively gift of nature
Coolness and peace your character
You come down with leisure
To water lives until they rapture

You goddess of life
Spread out in five
Carrying water in pipes
To enable a field to ripe

When in moderation you are a blessing
Making sights pleasing
With people ululating
And when in excess, lips part with cursing

I ENVY WATER AND AIR

Water does not die under any power
If you doubt, ask the scientist Director
Under high temperatures water becomes gas vapor
As for me with high temperatures I become earth favor

With low temperatures gain
Water changes into solid ice
As for me, my parts never recollect again
For I die never to set eyes on Jane
High temperatures on ice water pack
Will change it into liquid water as a matter of fact
But for me I shall never come back
Unless under a command of religious act

IMPORTANCE OF WATER

They call you water
Although you are colorless and tasteless a matter
All living things need you there
More than they need butter

You are formidable in eluding your enemies
When fire wants to destroy you, you change to gas fumes
And when winds want to blow you like sand dunes
You condense into a solid form

And when heat cracks you into mini cubes
You revert into a liquid
All these attempts are to make you die, they assume
Instead you teach them how to merry-go-around

WATER NEVER DIES

Water you are elusive in your realm
As such you never die like a ram
When they heat you warm
In order to inflict on you harm
You change into liquid form

And when they think
They will let you sink
By heating you more to pink
You change into a gas at a blink
And escape into air

When on air hanging
They cool you to thawing
In order to die freezing
You change into solid again
So hard to use a hand for breaking

When heating your solid status obtained
You change into liquid again
On the train to merry- go-round
In that way you escape death outright
Denying them their gain

I'M CALLED WATER

I'm called water
I'm present hither and thither
Above the soil and under
And surrounding the earth sphere

I enter every cell of living things
I move from one place to another at a blink
And from one form to another with wings
Either silently or with a force roaring

Sometimes I may be missed without trace
For my availability and form whereas
I'm always there blessed
Since creation I have never reduced or increased

CONQUEROR OF INJUSTICE (I)

Lucky, lucky oh life soother!
They call you water
So precious a matter
Every creature wonder
When they see you wander
In search of life to cater

But why this praises my friend?
What is special about my brand?
Am I different from other strains?
You must be flattering me down the drain
And an intended flattering is worst
Than genuine condemnation

Truly your nature at best
Is special on earth
It is different in length and breadth
From Adam and Eve myth
Whose cardinal sin after violating an oath
Has condemned all generations to death

DR. BELLARIO AHOY NGONG GENG

CONQUEROR OF INJUSTICE (II)

Your great parents so clean
Might not have committed so mean
Any sin to Almighty chagrin
That is why you with your kith and kin
Escape cardinal sin
And be able to avoid injustice down the lane

More over the ages
You do not die like wretches
Foremost to avoid smashes
You exist in three stages
Of solid, liquid and gases
To that human never matches

When injustice corners you at one stage
You move to the other page
Until it gets exhausted its rage
And disappears out like a mirage
In that you deserve a hot cake
For conquering injustice barrage

DOG

In all the animal kingdom
No animal is sharing home
So close with human than your name
And nothing will separate you come the doom

Your love with human is so tight
That you are misunderstood light
To have forsaken your rights
And surrender completely to human might

Little do they know about you
That towards the kindness you bow
But against human foe
You tear with forceful jaws

COW

You ancient companion of human
The first I saw you, I turned to run
Later I learned you were my second mum
Providing me with needs I want

Please receive my salutes
After making them jealous
When you give me without malice
Those tons of liquid to swell my wallets

To my family you have a central role
Which you play without fail
When we are old and unable to toil
With your milk we shall reach the goal

FOREST

At close look you are trees
Far away your green increases
Further you are like sentries
Forced to stand under duress

Your values are many
One day it was wet and sunny
At your midst we found honey
Which we ate selling some for money

Woe for a land without forest
It will be like farmers under arrest
Leaving their crops to pest
And to monkeys as honorable guests

SUN

In the sky you tower
The source of all power
Fixed in that position by the Knower
That vested it with energy to shower

Sun gives earth a purpose
To enable it expresses its fulfillment
Such as energy as well as life
Including human life and development

Life is not, without a sun
The time the sun will sink

The earth will be in ruin
And the moon will dance the same tune

AT THE MERCY OF THE SUN

Oh sun!
As your light on creatures has shown
And as you keep recharging land and moon
Life is at your mercy
Similar to that between a parent and son

Oh sun!
Without you, reigns doom
Darkness will loom
All earth will turn tomb
And life will have no room

Oh sun!
Nature forbids
As it has a wit
It will make it fit
To keep you in orbit

THE SUNSET HAZE

Facing west at half past six
Your imaginations are fixed
You will remember for weeks
Even though your memory is weak

Spectacular and beautiful
The designer was careful
As well as mindful
In capturing in full
The emotions of even the doubtful

Stand akimbo on high ground
To watch the yellow brown
On the horizon being drowned
Look! At the helix around
Like a King crown

MOON

Bride of the night
What makes you bright?
If you do not know it right
Sun will tell you live

Your bridegroom is a guy
Rotating at a distance high
When between it and earth you lie
The Earth briefly misses your husband eye

With moonlight we do not miss the sun
Hear children giggling with fun
Which they have concocted on their own
With joy they declared Garang has won

WIND

It was one evening day
I was going to a church to pray
The wind overwhelmed me on the way
I was swept to a nearby bay

I thought I was invited to a wind's home
Suddenly it formed a dome with foam
And up the sky it went, not to come
Leaving me forlorn as a tomb

My parents asked about the matter
I said I was chasing a wind
To enter her home softer
Which they greeted with laughter

AIR

At my nostrils I had a tingling feeling
Down I felt my chest yielding
Bowing and kneeling
To receive goddess of healing

Later I learned I cannot survive
Without five*
Each holding a knife
In few seconds it can erase life

Believe me when I tell
Air cannot be seen but felt

It can condense and melts
In its role to support life as well

*(air, sun, water, food, parents)

WATER MELON

With your shape and color
I thought you were a joker
So I placed you on a holder
And raised you up to fall asunder

To my surprise there fell on the ground
A material coloring reddish brown
It was so beautiful by all account
And so tasty to match nothing around

I collected your substance in a bowl
And together with my brother Paul
We galloped you down the bowels
How refreshing your substance to our soul!

CHICKEN

You are a bird by all creation
True bird without exaggeration
You flap wings without variation
And possess beaks for operations

Your crow heralds day break
And your production jolts an economic trick
Yet to the slaughter we have you dragged
Although with temerity you have jokes to crack

Even though you have wings to fly
And have other birds to ally
You chose to rely
On human so sly

For all birds that live with human
In their homestead and environs
You are the most valuable like sun
To a point of being taken for granted like moon

In you we get a cheap source of protein
The body needs for growth gain
And magicians use you to invite rain
As they use your body to cleanse and sooth pains

Whenever we hear your crows
We resoundingly raise our eye brows
Waking up to accomplish our work before morrow
In all without you we live in sorrow

HEN AND EGG MYSTERY

Hen and egg
Are two sides of one creation
On one side you see an egg
And on the other you see a hen

What exists first to produce the other make?
Is a mythical riddle pack

If it was a hen
Then what a fun
If there was no egg
And if it was an egg alone
Then what produces it
If there was no hen

Knowledge search stops there cold
Standing confused on cross road odds
Waiting for someone for a bailout
Wondering who will be the bailout lord
As this task is mind boggling
Only religion can provide an answer hidden in a divine code

THE MORNING BREEZE

One night it was humid and hot
The clouds on the sky loomed on spot
I thought I was in a cooking pot
Had it to continue, I was set to rot

At past mid night I guessed
I felt something cooling my chest
That put me at rest
And cuddled a deep sleep at best

At late morning I still had sleep arrears
When I woke up with a sneeze

I wondered what made me almost to freeze
They call it morning breeze

THE STILL NIGHT

The air filled with noises of all creatures
Acting under the demand of all pressures
In the fracas they suffer some fractures
The perpetrators have escaped to Mauritius

As the stars move westwards
All at the mid night is quiet
And no more could be heard
As if commanded by guards

How beautiful the still night
When calm reigns might
Even when you have a tongue bite
One can hear it at a kilometer height

USEFUL INSECTS (BEES)

How interesting is the nature
It does not need one to lecture
That some insects can harm faster
Ruining one's future

Some are innocently harmless
And so they exist countless
Others are nameless
With no harm they can live timeless

Yet others are extremely useful
They have the best model of rule
And their techniques of labor are whole
I'm presenting bees with a bull

BEES

They call us bees
Unlike cows that produce cheese
We do produce honey with ease
For work, we do not tease

But Alas! The honey we produce is both a blessing and a curse
Blessing, for we consider it a feeding source
A curse, for other creatures need it to fill their purses
Thus they rob us dry under our tears

We are surely at a crossroads
If we do not produce we die like toads
And if we produce we are at odds
With robbers carrying away our lot

BEES ON THE OFFENSIVE

We are tired each
Utterly tired like an eating dish
Of humans sucking us like leeches
Of our honey bliss
While no payback in earnest
Rendering us less rich

All what we do is to produce honey
From nectar of flowers shooting out of the body
And natural water down the valley
Nothing we take from humans' belly
Yet they rob us utterly
Of our precious treasure for money

From now on we are on offensive
We have orders to keep
From Her Majesty the Queen of Beehives
For our soldiers to sting to death never leave
All those humans' offspring of EVE
Tempering with our wealth and dashing our hopes

MAHOGONY

For a savannah, you are a native
Poising yourself massive
And takes people's minds captive
As they value you extensive

Your substance is so much typical
For most parasites it is fatal
From your timber, they prepare special
For use by top officials

How comfortable is your shadow
Once I entered your ghetto
To rest while listening to a radio
With no time, eyes got closed and I opened my jaw

TAMARIND TREE

You are a gift of nature
From high ground you rupture
Spreading roots wide for the future
And rising up a height to a measure

Your benefits are three
You count valuable among all fruit trees
And you provide strong building logs most people agree
As you provide your shadow for every one free

Look ahead with pride
And look behind with a content of a bride
That had your juice tried
And found that it was tastefully all right

BENEFITS OF A LALOOB TREE

A tropical tree with thorns all over
That produces tasteful fruit in winter
There is a hard seed cover
That protects the seed from robbers

The seed when pressed produces edible oil
Phosphates from burned twigs and leaves can season a meal
And proceeds from its durable timber can settle a bill
While young leaves are eaten during famine to save souls

All that is bitter is considered bad
But Laloob has proved that wrong

By presenting itself bitter yet
It is by all measures good

EBONY

Some people think black is evil
But you have proved them wrong double
By your black luster noble
And your strong shaft that makes it stable
So shiny I cannot resist admiring your table

Among trees of wonderful timber
You are special in a different way ever
As you are resistant to insects danger
I wish I find you in a dark corner
To elope with you a partner together

How wonderful you are Oh Ebony!
Our Chairman took you as his secret pony
Because you are also resistant surely
To eavesdropping of the enemy
Thank God, you are one of our liberators honey

MALARIA

You are a human enemy down a road
Since the ancient time slot
Stories of your evil plots
Are received without delight

All along you exploit human weaknesses
By striking at its poorest pages
Claiming millions of lives as your fire rages
All remedies you dismiss without vestiges

Recently humans have discovered your weak ties
You shy away when development shines
How long you may last to cut out lives
Not long before future generations on your grave dine

MOSQUITO

Look at your legs as you kneel
A small insect at acute angle tilts
Sucking blood at will
That is a mosquito at meal

It takes blood from a victim
In order to reproduce and multiply at whim
Leaving a person to suffer and die slim
To human kind millions who perished are a cream

How strange the nature operates
Human trade with money and bread
But mosquitoes go on trade
By exchanging disease with blood

INTESTINAL WORMS

To human judgment you are stupid
Because you feed on human meat to no limit
And when you eventually kill it
With it you are buried together with your kindred

You and humankind are riding on one horse
In relation to world environment
Human abuses environment to the worst
And the first to die of its rigors

Believe me both of you are deprived of your wits
How can you do what you did?
You cannot dine from a dish so clean bright
And use it also to collect your shit!

FISH

Fish you live in water
While we live on land better
But all of us depend on air in nature
And swim as we move like Saturn

Fish we eat you
And you eat us too
Depending on who has fallen low
On the other ones' jaw

Fish you are a source of a protein
Our body needs for growth gain

After we take your delicious dish clean
We enjoy a sound sleep devoid of a grinding pain

TALAPIA FISH PLEA

Hear my plea Oh Mighty of all Mightiest!
You made me beautiful among all fishes
And made my body scales and gills
To match your imagination wishes
To that I have no complaint hints

You sacrificed me a lamb to animal diet
As their delicious delight
Among all meals I wet appetite
Of those who are normal and greedy alike
To that I have no complaint to cite

But you made human and crocodiles devour my offspring
To that I complain bitterly with plea and plead to ring
Because they are endangering my existence Oh King!
Either you make me bitter to their tastings
Or remove me from creation tidings!

A DIALOGUE WITH A SNAKE

Interviewer:
"Why are you different from other animals?
Why you do not have legs and others have them all?
See how you move on the walls
Your body moves in a zigzag way with risk of falls"

Snake:
"That is why our kinds are called snakes
We do not have legs because they are fake
See how beautiful we move with grace
Our zigzag movement deludes our enemies on land and lakes"

Interviewer:
"Why are you an enemy to all animals?
All of them are upon your hole
As you are on their balls
Is it because you move carelessly without a goal?"

Snake:
"We are against animals that show enmity
We always try to avoid them completely
But some animals look for us to kill and even eat us without pity
In that way we are always on defensive ferocity"

Interviewer:
"You are right
But why do you kill human beings as you sight
While they are kind to animals including you
And they have sworn to take your enemies for a fight"

Snake:
"Our strategy is tit for tat
We bite to kill all human beings that show enmity hot
As for those who are friendly we do bite not
Because we have a strong smell to tell an enemy from a friend lot"

DR. BELLARIO AHOY NGONG GENG

WHEN EARTH BECOMES HELL

Earth becomes hell
When science scans the universe all
And discovers more other existing bodies
Better than earth

When everything for life needs
Are in abundance naturally
Not a product of work or trade deeds
And all creatures have no death to meet

And they live in harmony
Without wars or acrimony
God to be physically seen riding a pony
And is in control of all affairs lonely

WHEN EARTH BECOMES HEAVEN

Earth becomes heaven
When science proves infinity times eleven
That there is no other existence den
 Than earth the heroine

All other existences are stone dead
Revolving and rotating at endless rounds
With earth an island in their midst
Glowing green under intelligent gaze

And there are no lives in any form
Or if there are in any norm

They are of inferior clone
Than that on earth back home

THE VALLEY OF HOPE

Valley of the Nile River
Time immemorial our ancestors live in you ever
And we have continued to live with you here
Your bosom is laden with resources
As you are a livelihood and a joy giver
We know you as valley of hope driver

Valley of the Nile River
When rains rain never
And reserves of food are over
You tap the vast stores of your liver
For every one of us to glitter
We know you as the valley of hope

Valley of the Nile River
When everywhere is dry ever
And animals have no grass feeders
You provide grass as ever greener
And water to quench thirst fever
We know you as valley of grass hopper

DEATH

A strange visitor that robs people's lives
It comes to drain but not with a pipe

And returns to cut but not with a knife
The body to unseen particles not to revive

Feared when it is far
Welcome when it is near
The beneficiaries on earth hate it more
While those bothered, like it dear

Whatever is done to divert any event
To the effect you want
Death is a natural giant
To be avoided it can't

THE VALLEY OF DEATH

Valley of the Nile River
Although you have been providing hope proper
You have also provided disaster
And suffering for people competing forever
Over your resources reservoir
They know you as the valley of death giver

Valley of the Nile River
Most wars since immemorial thither
Have been fought at your bosom hither
And many dear sons and daughters
Have perished here from wounds and blisters
For that reason they know you as the valley of a doomster

Valley of the Nile River
Many people and animals have been drowned by your water

Leaving their relatives and owners shedding tears ever
To mix with your water as it flows yonder
For that reason they know you as the valley of life grabber

FIRE

I'm fire
I never get tired
Mixed with air
I tend to roar higher
With sand I tend to move lower

With care and carefulness of an elder
I serve you diligently
To achieve higher goals earnestly
However if you manage me carelessly
I shall rage havoc with wince and wails incessantly

Until you quench me with water
Do not think it can defeat me either
For even if water can calm my tongues
In the process I send it to air with hissing laughter
In short there is no winner and no loser

DIALOGUE WITH FIRE

Interviewer:
"Fire you are odd
Sometimes you are found in a smiling mood
Helping people to prepare their food

Sometimes you are an angry lot
Consuming everything below your boot

Fire:
"Surely if you do not understand me yet
You will not know to use me lad
In short carelessness makes me mad
And carefulness makes me humble to Dad
Both run the role of cat and rat"

Interviewer:
"I see ee ee ee ee ee ee ee ee ee
That means if I treat you like an enemy
You cause ravages and havoc to me
And if your mind and me agree
You will kiss me to my knee"

Fire:
"That is absolutely right honey
Some people spray me with water when I'm angry
What they do not know is that out of fury
I send water into the air to come with rain in a hurry
As for me my mother sun will refill my dairy"

DESERT

Necked part of the earth
How can we cloth you best
While cloths shy away in curse
When they see your nudity vast

Necked part of the earth
How can we water your thirst
While water escapes from your path
When they realize your vast dry length

Necked part of the earth
How can we feed your appetite lust
While food runs away in fright
When they see the hollow of your jaws so wide

SCORPION

You are small from an insect trail
But strong by the power spell
Of a poison hanging at your tail
It produces pains and wails
As if one is pricked by nails

This proves the Saying of a guy
It is power that matters
And not the size of a weapon
Otherwise a person should not be made to die
By viruses so small to be seen by naked eye

All animals whatever their weight
Shake with fear at your sight
And thus the great resolve to fight
And crash you to pieces
When on the way you meet

DR. BELLARIO AHOY NGONG GENG

SCORPION AND FROG IN A JOKE GAME

Scorpion and frog once on a lane
Had a light moment of joke alone
On who could inflict a serious pain
If they beat each other using their tails' canes
Each fixed its eyes on a game to win

Frog started first by giving scorpion lashes of ten
Allowing the scorpion to count from one to ten
The scorpion endured its lashes with count up to ten
Without flinch and wince at the end

When it was a turn for frog to receive lashes
It counted one to be ten lashes
Not ready to receive more lashes
For they were too painful touches
Thus the game was won over by one scorpion lash

EVIDENCE OF UNHEALTHY ENVIRONMENT

When flies swarm around
Whatever you eat they surround
Sometimes in your food they get drowned
In other they bath in it and get crowned
Know that your environment is unhealthy

When the air surrounding you stings
Holding your nose while eating
And feeling sick while waiting
Your friend on appointment dating
Know that your environment is unhealthy

When there is unsightly scene
Especially when socked with rain
In a place no one is responsibly keen
And you try to take action but in vain
Know that your environment is unhealthy

HEALTH

My name is Health or Wellbeing
Between me and you is a tight rope so thin to see
Which you must walk to reach me before retiring
Do not falter lest you fall before arriving

On reaching so nice
Your gift is a prolonged comfortable life
Wrap in a golden pipe
As our relation ripe

Here is a secret to mention
When you want to reach my mansion
Cancel you fashion
And live in moderation

LIFE IS WALKING ON A TIGHT ROPE

Life is walking on a tight rope
Even if we tie it to a hope
And bless it with prayers of Pope
Yet it is so thin we can't cope

If on one side we walk too fast
We may be driven to the other
And even on other side we grip a mast
Still we may barely survive
With feet hanging in the air

Whatever we develop
Down the slope
Including standing aloof
We shall one time plop

VISIBLE AND INVISIBLE

Visible is either huge or near
With your eyes you can hold dear
Invisible is either small or far
If you claim to see you are rare

Visible is weaker than invisible
Because it is made of many parts breakable
Invisible is small and stronger than visible
Because it is made of small parts indivisible

The visible has tendency to disintegrate
The component parts migrate
The invisible is stable and does not irritates
 Why they endure is nature's secret

ESSENCE OF LIFE

People exist to appreciate creation
With adequate attention
They should discover natural laws in operation
And to apply them without variation

Natural laws well applied bring comfort and long life.
Just as you go along with a happy wife
Enjoy a fresh fruit ripe
And indulge your nerves in extra nine

Natural laws applied wrongly
Leads to demise early
After paying dearly
For what you missed to do carefully

GOOD AND BAD

Good is what sustains human life
Treat it with respect and delight
Bad is what prevents human to live and thrive
Except when good is expected to arrive

Peace and long life are the benefits of good
As they are sanctioned by God
Suffering is the product of bad
Victims are trodden upon with boots

Good and bad are two faces of one coin
If there is no good, bad will not be known
And if there is no bad, good will not be grown
Both exist to provide knowledge to human kind

CHAPTER IV

POWER AND INSTITUTIONS OF POLITICS

CONSTITUTION

Mother of all laws
Like a milking cow
Produce your milk now
And deliver to your children's jaws

Do not say you are sick
For that will make your children weak
From seeping unhealthy milk
Although you were down for a week

When you are healthy you will endure
As the crooked lines of a contour

And when your feet are tender
There is no way to render

MY COUNTRY

The dearest I have on this planet
Say cheese for your smile to radiate
And receive a present of lemonade
That will be delivered to you by Janet

I had your wounds nursed
And when you were cursed
My anger burst
And shower you with verse

But when I was at my worst
And was crying with tears
You never had ears to hear
Although the power was yours

PARLIAMENT

I'm called parliament
I exist on people demand
My absence is a bad omen
For between people and Executive I cement

I'm all people power in diminution
Tyrants want to subject me to elimination
But democrats provide me with ammunitions
And protect me with lamination

Yet others want my name maimed
By giving me some model names
Such as playing a rubber stamp game
And being a toothless dog with no aim

EXECUTIVE

They call me Executive
I implement the parliament motive
And render all problems curative
To this work I'm a native

Sometimes I'm misunderstood
When I work with excited mood
People think I'm rude
And when I jump like a toad
They tread me with a boot

This makes me sometimes moody
With an iron fist I send people drowsy
Sweat, tears and blood mingle uncontrollably
At last they call me tyrant, as my hands are so bloody

ANGEL AND DEVIL WORLDS

When there are power groupings
People see two worlds emerging
One world hopping
And the other world limping

If one world is an Angel
The other is a devil
And if one is a devil
The other is an angel

Use common wit
To follow what is fit
Even if you sit
In unsightly pit

EFFECT OF HIGH LEVEL DECISIONS

If they give people benefits
People praise their Leaders great
With high pitched voices, they shout
Carrying them on their heads
And pressing them against their bosoms

If decisions are unpopular
People boo their leaders
With a thunderbolt pitch toner
Kick them with their feet harder
And press feet against their butts

Beware Oh Leaders in action!
To make decisions meeting people's emotions
Before you ink, gather their interest with dedication
For what you think is good for people as a nation
May be for them a poison

POWER AND RIGHT

Power is the common factor
If it was a tractor
And Victor a sick contractor
It would have carried him to a Doctor

When you have power even without right
Your claim prevails
When you have power with right
Even more the claim sails

But when you have less power although with right
You will lose even though you wag your tail
And if you have less power with no right
Your claim will never assume trial

This is the necked truth from sages
Power is the common factor throughout ages
As it reinforces another adage running pages
End justifies the means even if fire rages

WHEN ALCOHOL, LUST AND MONEY ARE SERVANTS OF KING LION

Once King Lion invited applications written by hand
From Alcohol, Lust and Money applicants
Because of their outstanding popularity in the land
To chose as he wanted
The one who will serve him better as a servant

DR. BELLARIO AHOY NGONG GENG

Alcohol said he would serve him best
When he is exhausted and tired up to his chest
From attending matters of state in earnest
By making him forget at least
About the weight of problems at his desk

Lust said he would tingle his nerves for ever
To cease and to pause never
Making him feel great and fresher
As after a bath with a shower
For variety, clients have to change after every hour
Only the sky will limit the power

Money said he is the master
Of the two servants waiting
As he could cause the King
To order them when straying
Or when reluctant to work at his wing

Convinced by statements though shallow
He decided to take them all at a go
And to be his bed fellows
He laid alcohol on the left side with stereo
Lust on the right and Money as a pillow

For long duration he enjoyed time like a bat
The result, he is in a state of stupor but not dead
Leaving the matters of state to hovering eagles, his guards
How shall his kingdom last my God?
Only time will witness his fate

FATE OF POLITICAL GROUPINGS

How great it is at the beginning
The group keeps convening
To crystallize and makes planning
Together they keep toasting and dinning

When gain is certain
Few would draw a curtain
And squander the whole gain
While having others restrained

Clique will be paid in gold
And majority paid in doll
Fortunes of some will be upheld
While others will hang on a pole

YOU ARE STRANGE MY COUNTRY

When you are under chains
Inflicted with pains
You need all of us to free your hands
In consequence martyrdom is obtained

When you are being protected
From being desecrated
You need all citizens to have defense erected
Any alien intervention is seriously rejected

But when you produce milk
Ready for a fill

Only a handful benefit at will
Leaving others struggling to get a meal

POLITICAL JUSTICE DILEMMA

You grant political rights today
To political activists on a golden tray
In order to keep grievances at bay
And uproot vestiges of dismay
So as to usher in peace to stay

They will encircle and bow
Plunder public wealth between your eye brows
Stop all the progress by bending the law
And turn people against you
Before they take your seat by fueling the row

If in case you deny over night
Their political rights
By making everything tight
And keeping security to the ground tied
To prevent opposition to bite

They will kick you with their legs
Until you vomit an egg yolk
Before they bind you with a yoke
And hang you by the neck
As they have the powers take

LEGACY OF A DEAD LEADER

A dead leader is sent over
To rest with mixed tears
Some toast with beers
As they have settled their arrears

And some have hearts laden with fears
For the love one they dear
To tingle public ears
His directives are geared

To last for some years
After that their works are jeered
To shreds they tear
As time away wears

DEMOCRACY

Rule of the people by the people
Tyrants wish you toppled
But your strength kicked them double
Then they try to render you feeble
But you emerge robust and able

Beware of hypocrites
Who say they follow your creed
But turn to have you treaded
Who say your philosophy they read
And on the way they leave it on a road

You are a pearl mankind has ever conceived
Never get deceived
By those running with jeep
For a short distance they will stumble on a heap
Leaving you smiling with EVE

THE FALSE LIBERATOR

A false liberator
Have two personalities in nature
In one personality order
He fights for a cause better
And can be persecuted by enemy directors
Prosecuted and even wounded by enemy rulers
That he does to draw attention of sympathizers

On the other Personality
He loves power and wealth with intensity
To extent of embracing criminality
Or condoning corruption in totality
Cling to power unjustifiably
And can engage in injustices deeply
Forgetting he fought against these vices vigorously

A false liberator is easy to tell
He has two tongues in his mouth hole
One tongue is connected to a bell
He articulates the cause well
Those convinced by his heroism kneel
The unwary following the trail
Can be confused by this tactics style

On the other tongue
He contradicts himself with speed
For whatever he says
Although it lands to ears sweet
He throws something out with spit
More worst than a bull shit
As one can fertilize a farm with it

DEMOCRACY THE ULTIMATE GOAL

Even if you make Monarchy or Autocracy glitter
Encouraging artists to flatter
Reduce all liquids to sell a cent for a liter
And make builders to deliver
Democracy is the ultimate goal

Even though you change Oligarchy or Dictatorship to Gold
And make Mena from the sky fall
Causing monolith to roll
Commanding winds to hold
Democracy is the ultimate goal

Although you emerge all the systems to one
Other systems will set with the sun
Rising in the morning with their back bent
Leaving democracy to elope with beautiful Ann
Because Democracy is the ultimate goal

GOOD AND BAD RULER
(A dialogue between Mr. Inquisitive and Mr. Wise)

Mr. Inquisitive
"I wonder who is a good and a bad ruler?
I searched the entire world to the polar
Never did I find an answer better
Than the one here
I do not expect your answer lower"

Mr. Wise
"Look for which category is satisfied by the decision of a ruler
If the populace, you are near a good ruler
And if the top brass, you are straining under a bad ruler
Do not be taken in by a racial color
For a ruler has no color"

Mr. Inquisitive
"But if both categories are satisfied by a ruler
Because of the treatment fairer
Nobody is junior
And no one is senior
All are of the same status like molar teeth"

Mr. Wise
"If both accept the ruler
The ruler must be god in miniature
May not be among the world dwellers
But may be descending our solar system
Coming from the part of the universe queerer"

PREROGATIVE OF A SOVEREIGN

Institutions can prepare laws by section
But a sovereign will put them in action
He controls a country as the forest is to a lion
And holds no less in his hand than a red iron

He lives above laws
The top surface being smooth like roses
While he avoids the undersurface rows
Because they are sharp like saws

He takes decisions finale
As there is no one above his nails
And can abuse anyone under his tail
And gets a smile response instead

A LEADER

A leader takes people with a balloon
Using tactics drawn
From vision he owns
He recruits both clones and clowns

Some suffer great loss
Because they have inflicted most
Some entertain great bliss
As they did not gather moss

A leader is both loved and hated
Since he wears two hats

When he dies fated
Mix tears of loss and relief mingle unabated

FATE OF A DESPOTIC SOVEREIGN

He makes laws
Subject them for vows
And push them down to people with his toes
Because they are too sharp to cut like knives

When people have enough under strain
They feel their trust has been betrayed
Threatening the crown to be derailed
Especially when his train is for a long time on a rail

They march enough is enough his mighty weight
Which they have carried for four times eight
From today for day and night
No monster can delay their right

COST AND BENFITS OF LIBERATION

Oh! Citizens yearning for a free country
Come in a group of two times three
And wait for me under that fig tree
To tell you this bitter fact free

Liberation cost is borne by all
As it is too expensive for few to pay
While benefits are for elite in control
Any grumbler will go to hell

Do not hope for a return for what you give
For nature has prepared it in heaps
But think of how to return what you receive
For people are waiting with passions high

THE DEMISE OF THE LIBERATORS

As the liberation process moves on
Liberators are united and act like ants
Sticking together as they can
To achieve goals as one

When freedom is achieved
Leaders differ deep on who is to be a chief
On invitation of the winner former opponents arrive
Leaving the losers to weep and wag a bitter hand wave

As time goes on former opponents shed their colors
They entrench themselves deep like teeth molars
And sing songs of liberators
Signaling the political demise of former liberation actors

FREEDOM WHERE ARE YOU?

You told me a location of your abode
I set myself on a road
With sweat and blood I searched the woods
But you were on nowhere to note
Where are you?

You mentioned achievement date
With patience I waited my fate
Finally I reached the gate
But you were not there in wait
Where are you?

You said you have a body
I saw a mirage of you already
But that was a folly
For you were not there in reality
Where are you?

DIALOGUE BETWEEN MR. INQUISITIVE AND MR. FREEDOM FIGHTER

Mr. inquisitive
"Mr. Freedom fighter
How is it that you are left out thither?
From sharing the freedom cake
As reliable stories indicate hither
You were in the center"

Mr. freedom Fighter
"Mr. Inquisitive we are revolutionaries equal
But those who are more equal fill their bowels
They have a mouth mess to be wiped with a towel
 And those less equal have empty bowls
They have to complain with a cry of an owl"

Mr. Inquisitive
"Mr. Freedom fighter this is a bitter lesson

If many people know this reason
They will not join struggle for liberation
As they will leave it to owners of mansions
And drivers of V8 Toyotas and Nissans"

Mr. Freedom Fighter
"Mr. Inquisitive, there are those who sacrifice for others
Irrespective of what they materially gather
Their pay is rhetorical speeches of praises
Especially when they are silent in their graves
Which dissipate with wind as time goes"

POLITICIANS

There are two groups of politicians
As they float like a boat in the middle of an ocean
Swaying here and there according to conditions
Yet they are under the driving force of ambition
They wait for opportunity to spring into action

One is called self interest crop
They wear public interest coats up to their ear lobes
Ostensibly not to be known by mob
They wait for a chance to throw out the coats and rob
Majority fall among this elusive group

The other is called public interest group
Wearing a public interest ring
They serve public without eye blink
Their intentions are there for the public to ink
Minority if any fall under this group

DESPOT HAS NO COLOR
(A dialogue between Mr. Inquisitive and Mr. Wise)

Mr. Inquisitive
"Does color make a difference to a despot?
I mean do white and brown have the same attitude
As yellow and black despotic lot
Or do they board different boats?"

Mr. Wise
"Your question is wise
When influence of power arise
They apply the same vices
Towards their subjects"

Mr. Inquisitive
"I mean does a color make a difference?
Does a white despot
Give their subjects just political dispensation
Better than the brown, yellow or black ones?

Mr. Wise
"Whatever their color
Influenced by their just culture
When they drink the same alcohol of power
They become despotic and a despot has no color

POLITICS
(Blind, deaf and selfish)

Three persons boasted they know
What politics are, they vow
One said it is blind to a humane law
Because it does not see poor people below
Straining when hunger gnaws

The other said it is deaf silent
Because it does not hear people on road bend
Demonstrating in quest for free hand
Or hear children requesting in a poem meant
For education to reach their end

The last said it is selfish
Because its leaders live as they wish
Making themselves rich
And get use as they please
To an extravagant life on a beach

Who among them is right?
As they are all logically tied
Since these are three aspects of a monolith might
Subjecting any description to a slight
Can be justice denied

POWER SO SWEET

So sweet and intoxicating
Even if satisfied they keep eating

The effect of the alcohol fitting
As it can drive them to blood letting

Soil so fertile to breed hatred at home
Instability and disunity constitute a time bomb
Wars and revolutions the outcome
Driving away boom out of Rome

Only GOD fearing holds it in moderation
By shortening the duration
To reduce the risk of treason
Better leave the rest for admiration

OFFICE OF POLITICS

Office of politics has a table made from pieces
Of different sizes and shapes
Where politicians sit to discuss issues
In a spirit of give and take as their interests match
The aim is to have a win-win situation crowned with golden stitches
But usually some give less than can be sucked by leeches
Or give more than expressed in speeches

It has a chair to host
A referee at any cost
And regulates topics that arose
As well as speeches of bosses
When they agree they throw a toast
But when they disagree at most
They push it in a dustbin below a table cloth

At the end
They either carry them to the garbage pit
As they rant
Or burn them in an incinerator den
Or push them to a committee
As committees in essence
Are exhaust pipes of politicians

RIGHTS ARE FOR THE STRONG

Hear politicians making a row
Rights are for everyone a state owes
And hear lawyers echoing under a vow
Stating that no one is above the law

The reality speaks clear and loud
Conveying a different message aloud
Not by words dressed with cloud
But by deeds and practices tried

Rights are for a strong party
In any given society
The strong enacts them into laws
And live above them in entirety

SOLUTION OF A COUNTRY PROBLEMS BY DIVISION

When a country sustains an injury
People usually jump to a division in a hurry
As a golden solution to a problem they carry
Closing away other solutions in a granary

Not knowing that problem thither
That divides do not become smaller
By the division of the country hither
What becomes smaller is the size proper

However the problem master
The same as the former
Only changes from one person to another
And causing the same effect ever

REVOLUTIONS AND THEIR FATE

Revolutions are made by the braves
And enjoyed by those playing safe
The brave cannot enjoy the grapes
As they are already in the grave

While safe players like scavengers, thrive
As they pick up fruits of a revolutionary drive
Because the brave does not live to strive
And to wait for the fruits of their labor to arrive

The only dividend they win
Is a title of a hero or heroine
And a commemoration of a martyr day there in
Amid tears rolling from the eyes of kith and kin

WORRY ABOUT THE BABY (NATION)

Many years of struggle for you
For your sake there was a bitter row
As we all know
We were slaughtered like cows

Now that you are born
Which we welcome with blowing horns
But some want to welcome you with thorns
And receive you with a towel torn

You are the only baby
That makes everyone happy
No one was born before your day
And no one will be after your stay

REINSTATEMENT OF A TYRANT

When a tyrant whose rule has gone on
Unscrupulously for a long time run
Is reinstated for another ruling bond
Two opposite emotions occur in one person

One dislike the occasion proceeding
As it is merely extending his suffering
But difficult to express his feeling
For fear of punishment

Another is pretending happiness cheers
Congratulating a tyrant as he vows for other years

This is betrayed by internal feeling of hate arrears
Causing hate tears to flow as happy tears

A STAIGHT STICK IS CROOKED IN WATER

Do not praise a person in a hurry
When he is not a public figure yet
For he is presenting to you merely
One side of the character story
That is always bright and flowery

Reserve praise until when
He has ascended a throne
Where conditions will force him down
To expose both sides of the character coin
And both good and evil have acted and gone

You may be surprised to discover
That the person you admire dearer
When he is a lay person proper
Is not the same one when in power
For a straight stick is crooked in water

EXHORTATION FOR NATIONAL UNITY

All people of my dear country
With all your creeds and faiths in diversity
Bustling in your various degrees
Of ethnic sanctuary
And leaning on the facts of your history

You may be holding keys
Of different political views
And divide yourself like fleas
Into different political parties
Chasing each other for power bliss

However you should have one value core
A common denominator to mirror
Unity, unity and unity and only unity no more
For although cows are of different colors like flowers
All of them produce milk with one white color

WHETHER POLITICS ARE GOOD OR BAD

Politics are good when they serve public glory
In terms of giving people goal acuity
And solving their problems diligently
With spices of fairness and a taste of equity

They become bad when they are ploy concoctions
As a cover up to serve individual dimensions
People are left in a confused situation
And this provides recipe for turmoil and revolution

Beware of promises during elections rounds
Politicians make these promises storms
In order to be elected for another term
For vows made in storms are forgotten in calms

COUNTRY AND RULERS

In a country where rule of law dwells
The ruler works at ease with no troubles to quell
He enjoys his job cursing no one to hell
And a country progresses and prospers as well

When a ruler intimidates by coercion
A country will serve him alone to his satisfaction
And slides to dictatorship of one's concoction
Never to recover unless under a revolution

When a ruler is being intimidated
Its tantamount to being beheaded
He loses the control of a power mandated
And a country slides down a hill defeated

ADVICE TO EARS THAT CAN HEAR

When people who have not been grumbling
Are at aloud complaining
Back up by demonstrations of their offspring
And even with some clashes and rumblings
With security forces opposing

Thank God and hurry
For a solution to a fury
There is chance to avoid injury
For what harms most and difficult to bury
Is what is not talked about in a rally

But when people who have been complaining
Suddenly stop from grumbling
Then prepare for Tsunami to be coming
For far in the sea a trouble storm is gathering
With terrific speed it is striking

POWER CYCLE IN A GIVEN SYSTEM

Come and look into a microscope of history tales
Take one power cycle and observe the details
In one band of the spectrum scale
You will see a strong leader being hailed
And welding power with confident and charisma unprecedented

Watch how he would select his subordinates
He prefers weaklings and sycophants under rates
In order to make them as his aides
As he will push them like buttons to tick his dates

When these under rates eventually take over power
They continue appointing the same button bearers
Until the setup enters into dark tunnel corner
Consequently the stars appear again with sheers
And the cycle pattern continues further

That means in the whole power game scenarios
There will be few star leaders series
And many sycophant leaders periods
Bravo, bravo sycophants' leaders

DR. BELLARIO AHOY NGONG GENG

PEOPLE, LEADERS AND POWER

Squat, hop and squeak
Think and understand as quick
How power of people ticks
Under manipulation of leaders clique
When power is sinking to a pit
Leaders play safe their wits
And mobilize people to salvage it
Embracing pain and martyrdom summit

When it is secured properly
Only leaders practice it discriminately
Leaving people kicking their heels nervously
And licking their wounds incessantly

POWER IS A POLITICAL ALCOHOL

Power like alcohol intoxicates
By replacing friendship with hate
Brotherhood also fades
At the behest of newly recruited mates

New acquaintances will occupy seats
They pat their backs as the powerful ate
New titles are sir and madam and old names will be odd
As they are considered abusive and belated

Welcome to a house will be done at a gate
Issues taken with good humor will be for debate
And end up as power dictates
Any previous agreement will be there to wait

TO BE A NATIONAL HERO

If you want to be a national hero
The carrier of bow and arrow
Receiving salute like a pharaoh
 And walking through saluting kangaroos

You must climb a ladder summit
By aiming your weapon to hit
Your fellow nationals on their heads
And subdue them to retreat

Arriving at national level
You will continue with two struggles
Fighting national notables
As well as protecting a nation from external evil

THE FAVORITES OF A LEADER

They always stay around a leader net
Protecting him from public threat
As well as providing his daily bread
These are the same people who keep his secrets
 Poising as loyal and die hearts

If affairs are good everything runs a speed of light
But if there is a crack a leader is in a dilemma
If he sends them away they will expose the weak side
And if he keeps them they pull him down the drain
As all of them will fall in a political hole so wide

Keep them at arm guard
And do not let them access your heart
For they are the same blood
With your professed enemies
Less the distance from you, Dad

ABSOLUTE POWER

I'm absolute power
I have no father or mother
Or brothers or sisters
In short I have no relatives ever
And I do not need them to prosper
Why do I bother?
While they put my throne in danger

In all, I need breathing buttons only
Those who can laugh when I laugh candidly
And be angry when I'm angry even unjustifiably
And dance when I dance emotionally
They need not be relatives to be treated tenderly
But those who can kiss and wash brilliantly
Any part of my body I desire fondly

If anyone wants to topple me from my dynasty
I would send him ahead to eternal life city
Before I join with my kitty
But shall I really join? Unless I doubt my integrity
Because Creator assured me in totality
That I shall live forever, no need for eternity
As I'm his image on earth, His new eternal locality

POWER DYNAMICS

Power is so sweet I bet
To those rendering nothing to a state
Bothersome and uncomfortable a seat
To those concerned with the problems in wait
As they grapple with what affect people fate
Nights become longer with debate
And days become shorter with queues at the gate

As problems are thick like cloud
It is better to hand them over in a boat
Than keeping them with you on board
At the end the problems notoriously
Reach accord with people to force you out
The sweetness of many years in no doubt
In one day is turned bitter with a spill of blood

As power is dynamic like pendulum
Oscillating between home and tomb
It is logical to quit when in boom
Than when in gloom
Pass on this advice Tom
Wise leaders always get ready before the danger looms
Foolish ones pay heavily at the gate of doom

LEADER, PEOPLE AND TRUST

They call me trust by God
Sometimes confidence is my code
Like the umbilical cord

That links mother to her child before lord
I'm the rope that binds taut
A leader with people under his court

When I'm in a healthy state
People trust their leader at high rate
He becomes credible as a master maid
They give him their support and mandate
A leader in return loves his people as his fate
Lies marooned under their shade

When I'm cut like electric current
As when a leader employs untrustworthy agent
People refuse to run for his errands
Hell gates open large with a torrent
And mistrust my rival, emerges as a tyrant
He had been imprisoned in hell under warrant
When I was intact and vibrant

Now streets litter with bodies of giants
Those who made the leader shined
But of late they wanted him cut in nine
The end is that mistrust controls the scene
He sends thousands and even millions to the Rhine
And at the end they send their leader to guillotines

RUNNING OUT OF A REVOLUTIONARY STEAM

At the beginning of the uproar
There is revolutionary vigor
Problems are stated on the floor

With articulation difficult to ignore
People hold their breath much more
And place esteem respect at their door
Surrendering them affairs in store

When objective is achieved at length
The former master hands over in perfect health
The miraculous stick of power across the breadth
In fact the stick of injustice on earth
Half of its shaft from below is red since birth
And is made of power girth
And the other half is white and made of wealth

As he uses this stick as a bible
For he cannot avoid its approval
The revolutionary steam for survival
Runs out and evaporates to avoid trouble
For it cannot stay stable
With power and wealth couple
As they are staunch enemies and rivals

HOW TO GAIN POWER

Some through force of arms get
As this is the shortest cut
They do not hesitate to fatally hit the target
To enable them display might

Others by popular approval they come
With music and pomp
Like sweet smell of Mom
They leave behind a good name

Yet others by playing cards they ascend
Canny tricks they present
With no efforts they drive Nissan
As they defy all voices of dissent

FREEDOM ELABORATED

Who says freedom! Freedom!
Means being free from problems
So that one leads a life full of pomp
And do whatever at whim

If that was true
All people through
Would be a swimming crew
In paradise the creator grew

Freedom means to be free
From someone handling your problem trees
He places them on your shoulders to carry
To his delight and glee

ARDENT FREEDOM SUPPORTER

I love freedom, my own
For the happiness it brings
So that I work for my things
For a living and that of my offspring
And wear dignity and self respect ring
Chose freely who ever will be ruling

As they will be fair and trust bearing
For they belong to my racial clique
They will not tie my voice with string
When I advise them not to swing
And they will not let my wealth shrink
When it is under their caring link

But Mister, you are looking down
At one side of freedom coin
On the other side under a throne
And hiding to prey on what you yearn
Are your trusts worthy barons
Bearing skin color like your own
They will pelt your freedom with stone
Squander your wealth before dawn
And render you a poor wretch forlorn
Resulting in losing up to your groin
The dignity you have meticulously sewn
On your integrity crown

Nonsense, I do not care at all
If I'm enslaved through my own yield
For when my leaders in exercise of their role
Have achieved their goal
I throw up a celebratory ball
If they amass wealth as a whole
I feel wealthy even if I'm a wretch soul
When they are happy behold
I'm also happy and bold
For when they belch
As a result of their full bowels
It will be enough to enjoy a smell

DR. BELLARIO AHOY NGONG GENG

DIVISION IS A FUNCTION OF INTEREST, IT HAS NO END

Divide, divide and divide and you will continue to divide
Until you become exhausted and surrender to tide
No problem can be solved by division right
Because division triggers more division wide

Division is a function of an interest of a clique
In order to achieve selfish end trick
Not knowing that when a stage so to speak
Has been set to divide and divide
It will continue to infinity without break

To give any problem a best solution
Look for justice and equity option
But being too bright some people offer rejection
As they are used to darkness of division
Since bright light will put them out of vision

TASTE OF POWER

Why do leaders start as democrats?
And when they get power and bread
They do not want to leave it fat
And when pressured hot
They wear dictators' hat
Scaring every opponent with threat
Chasing them left and right like cat and rat

What is the correct taste of power?
I'm confused and stunned for ever

Sometimes I thought it tastes sweeter
As evident from joy of leaders
Then later it turns bitter
As some leaders grind their teeth in pain tighter
How can one question have two opposite answers?

Your analysis is right my dear
Leaders start democrats before they can veer
Because they do not know the taste in here
And comfort it produces there
When on the throne they taste it deliciously rare
And for that reason they refuse to have it shared
To extent of turning dictators and being feared

It turns bitter when people react with stones
To their dictatorship and pull them down
With sweat and blood at dawn
In conclusion John
Power has cocktail of tastes of its own
From sweet to bitter zones
With other tastes interlaced in between

It is this blended taste of power snip
That coxed Adam and Eve
To commit the cardinal sin deep
Logically offspring keep
And let this power gene slip
From one generation to another in heaps
Until when the human era sleeps

DR. BELLARIO AHOY NGONG GENG

THE KING MAKER

Who is this person with a back bent?
To whom Prime Ministers and Presidents
Kings, Emperors, and Popes lend
Standing ovation with no relent
And shiver at his presence
Why is he so powerful without a dent?
Yet he has no official portfolio to represent

You mean you do not know? Come on Jim
He is his Majesty the King Maker without him
Prime Ministers would not be Prime Ministers at whim
Presidents would not be Presidents untrimmed
Kings would not be Kings how frequent they dream
Emperors would not be Emperors without his scheme
And Popes would not be Popes even when they catch a glimpse

He is so accurate in identifying the needs of a leader
And works to address them appropriately and in order
I tell you what Mister?
Come nearer to get a whisper
Lest others passing by eavesdrop it further
"Since he knows all the state secrets with some scenes darker
Tempering with him will cause a bloody nose to the owner"

ON DEFENSE OF POLITICAL NAIVETY

Nonsense! Why make those loud jeers
About politics staggering down the stairs
Do you expect a child born with no skill at all?

To reason and behave like the older peers
And like an adult of yester years?

Politics like living things are born to grow
And to advance to maturity row
For so many early years it must consume and borrow
While what it produces is zero
Still it cries louder for what it consumes tomorrow

At later years under oath
And to safeguard power and wealth
It allows others to experience a cocktail taste
While hiding the formula of cocktail birth
As power! God forbids, should not be shared on earth

LEADERS THAT BARK AND HOWL WITHOUT ACTION

A leader is a holder of command banner
Because he can give orders
And things happen in spite of a barrier
When he approaches commoners
People stand up with cheers
And in ovation that puts him on airs
I want to be a leader

That is good ambition Mary
You know what honey?
All of us want to be leaders
But not all leaders are starry
And respected personality
You better know them as they vary
So that you are not caught unwary

The successful ones are shrewd like sharks
Predicable and transparently stark
The disgraceful are oppositely dark
Quite notorious in igniting corruption sparks
These are leaders that bark
And howl without action and respect at work

FREEDOM IN FOCUS (I)

Is this what freedom is all?
Why I'm exception to a rule?
Still I'm hungry and sick to the soul
And my children are not going to school
I thought freedom would mean a goal
Free from every pain and discomfort as a whole
Everything falling like Mena cool
From our government wealth pool

No, No my dear
There are two types of freedom in the list
Total freedom in all accounts is limitless
The one being enjoyed by wild life in forests
This runs on the bases of the survival of the fittest
To survive one must be agile and strongest
Life is uncertain at worst
And its quality is sinking fast

There is relative freedom
Chosen by human before Rome
As they began to roam
It is not an individual freedom come

But under a collective name
Where few top leaders get a boom
Life can be comfortable or meet doom
Depending on type of leaders at home

FREEDOM IN FOCUS (II)

If they are nationalistic and capable
Life is good and noble
And if they are selfish and evil
Life becomes uncomfortable
I believe I'm suffering double
In a system horrible
Being managed below a table
By leaders with minds unable

That is right, I admire
I must be under a group selfish to share
But what can I do, my situation is dire?
Years back I rebelled against this system
With a hope that I would be free like a wild fire
It became a change of master for another heir
How can I manage the latest one sir?
I'm exhausted and tired

I need not manage it myself in the oaks
One day my offspring will shake off the yoke
There are two ways in vogue
To handle bad rulers in the dock
Either I strike between their eyes with a knock
Or I strike between their buttocks

I need not tell the rest under the hooks
Because I have experience with my dogs

PRAYERS OF SELFISH LEADERS

Publicly they pray
For people to be free
Silently they ask Almighty to agree
To let them rule for generations three

Openly they pray for people to prosper
Deep in their hearts they want to be rich ever
And powerful like Ceaser
Minus his death bitter

Publicly they want their systems to stay longer
Silently they want to avoid all danger
Surrounding themselves with gunners
And wish to stay healthy and younger

LIBERATION GOAL PATH

A path to a liberation goal
Is not a straight line at all
It takes a zigzag course on a hill
 And follows a thin line tied to a nail

Because it is thin some stumbles to the right
Others attempting to balance make it to the left side
Some think they have reached the goal height

Others think that it is too far from sight

If it was a straight line and smooth
It would not take a long time for a truth
To be realized through the grinding of teeth
And bleeding of nose

THE RULE OF FORCE

When force rules brute
Tramping the ground with its heavy boots
And opening its wide mouth
In preparation mode
To swallow anything en route

Justice flies out of the wall crack
Its tail stuck between its hind legs
And running for its life sake
Lest he will be put on stake
Its remains to be packed in a sack

Justice sanctuary will be the religious institute
While wearing religious attire to cover suits
He will be crying out for help from mutes
One person can however hear him aloud
And that is the same force that made him destitute

DR. BELLARIO AHOY NGONG GENG

PEACE AND WAR

Peace and war are two opposite faces of one coin
Peace is continuation of war without using weapons
War is continuation of peace with weapons talking aloud
They are inextricably intertwined in a shroud
That if you stop one the other will pop out

Thus the saying goes as this
When you are at war
Then prepare for way to peace
And when you are in peace bliss
Then prepare for war please

Some people relax when they are at peace yard
So long so that war can get them unprepared
These are people who quiver at heart
Vomit and swallow their vomits curd
When war is forced on them not prepared

GOING ON AN ERRAND

My Master one time sent me for an errand
To go to a planet appearing beautiful
And spherically green in the telescope
To study how people there
Govern them selves

After many years of study flow
Three groups run the planet below
One is a group of few bulldozers crew

In power they wallow
As they give orders and others are to follow

The other group is the many sycophants' toasters
That follow the bulldozers blindly even on nonsense
They do not analyze orders lest they would be losers
The other group is formed of few critics
That criticizes the orders of the bulldozers

Listen Oh people! And take a gentle note as you discern this lesson
In that planet powerless critics will never rule
As long as the powerful bulldozers pull
And use sycophants as tools
Unless they join a sycophant pool

In that day a great war of competition will fill airs
And embrace all the sycophants for years
Splitting the planet into minute asteroids bursts
Only our planet will be shinning in the whole universe
Are you happy Master Mars?

WHEN TWO ELEPHANTS FIGHT

When two elephants are fighting fiercer
It is the ground that determines the winner
The one standing on hard ground firmer
Will definitely win over
Than the one standing on ground softer

Prepare the ground with concrete
Oh Elephant! If you want to succeed
Now and in future treat
Otherwise you run a risk so great
Of losing a battle because of greed

The battle to power house prison
Where ground is painted crimson
And servants present none
Other than unprovoked smile in unison
With your entry to a pavilion

POWER IS A FACTOR

No! No! No! Colleague
Are you surprised really?
That an incompetent at the hill peak
Is calling a competent one weak?
Come on! Let your sense click
And observe this equation kicking

Incompetent person, all sages ignore
Plus power, changes to competent orator
And competent person in décor
All sensible people adore, without power
Changes to incompetent poor
In other words power is a factor

But how do you get power in this land?
When all options are closed in Heaven
Turn your brain around

And lift it up with your hand
The answer is hidden
Underneath Eden

THE NECESSITY OF LEADERSHIP CHANGE

Leaders tend to remain in power forever
Because the position makes them towers
Allowing them to become world rovers
And constitutional and legal robbers

Even if a leader is great
It is still necessary to quit
To allow others to lead
And taste the sweetness of fruit

Continuous leadership is boring
There is necessity for leadership change
Yet popular demands, they keep ignoring
Leaving people on streets roaring

HOW LEADERS LOSE

At the beginning of their career
People are all dear
They beckon them near
And offer their ears to hear

How different when long in power
You cannot approach them unless through a bower

And will not know you unless through a knower
As you will not get supported unless you lower

When he drops again
He feels the pain
And would want to regain
But all in vain

LEADERSHIP RIVALRY

Those in power like to stay long
To fatten their account in the bank
Those out of power take them wrong
They would like to sound a gong
And have them hanged

When the rivals come to power
They forget the past faster
Entrench themselves deeper
Become hatred growers
And peoples' mowers

What then is the way out?
If you do not want the situation growing hot
And earth echoing with heavy boots
With sky laden with thick soot
Allow democracy to brood and to have roots

LIVING WITH POWER GIANTS

Living with power giants, you are a dwarf
Between them you produce a gap
Which they can use to lay a map
Forgetting your presence they place barbs

In other occasion you are a servant
Can be sent to run an errand
Approaching them you have to bend
In order to get a favorable hand

At worst scenario you are a ball
Being kicked here and there until you fall
And if you cannot sell
You are thrown to hell

A WARLORD

To achieve ends so far
He adopts war
To clear obstacles that bar
His interest to become a star

Public interests are but a story
This can be mentioned in oratory
Bordering flattery
And to justify victory

His options are two
Either he dies in a coup

Or he takes power by his jaw
Leaving people to watch in awe

I STOOD IN AWE

For food a young lion went hunting
Every day it went around and found nothing
The big one came mounting with a catching
And fed the young one up to red lining

The young grew strong with vigor
Under the protection of a figure
With characteristics of a tiger
Differences were relegated since they were meager

Alas! When the big lion on the river bowed
In order to drink it's due
The young strong lion jumped and gnawed
On its neck until it fell dead at its jaws

Not remembering the good the big lion showed
Because such types of acts are few
And while I was watching through a dew
I stood in awe!

SELFISHNESS IS STRONGER THAN NATIONALISM

My good leader once told me
When he prevails to be
He must act like a bee

And make fairness a key
To open the eyes of justice to see

When the time came to prevail
He succumbed to vile
By employing one who hailed
From his kinship trail
Attempts to persuade him failed

In fact only few can conjure individualism
Because it is much rooted than nationalism
In every cell of constitutionalism
From there emerges realism
Self interest is stronger than nationalism

QUEER ARE HUMAN BEINGS!

Queer are human beings!
In justice they hate
And to avenge they trample the perpetrators gate
But alas! The same people who hate injustice state
On being influential apply it on other mates

Queer are human beings!
Corruption they deplore
When others practice it, they abhor
But when they have a floor
They out do it glare

Queer are human beings!
When a rich play guest

They are served free of charge to their best
But when a poor presents himself to a host
They ask him to meet a cost

HOW CLEVER THEY ARE!

They tell you to kneel down
And close your eyes tight
In reverence to Creator Crown
But when you open your eyes to count
Your wealth has been looted at dawn

They tell you they are democrats
From now on no rights will be degraded
But underneath they allow single rule to operate
They tell you corruption they abhor at any rate
But on the table at home they honor it great

They swear nepotism cannot be ordained
All what it brings is injustice and pain
But all around are friends and relatives entertained
They claim they are born again
But what they do evokes delight for a devil to regain

WHAT POWER IS LIKE

Power is not like air
If it was, it would have been here and there
Everyone would access it anywhere
Rivalry and revolutions would not occur

Power is not like water
If it was, it would widely be available in nature
Majority would have it on alter
Few would struggle to get it there

Power is like a ball
Every player wants to score a goal
While some struggle to wrestle it out all
Others to the bottom of their voices yell

EDUCATED PERSON DISEASE

Intoxicated with power
And without another power to restrain
Educated person turns a dictator
Around him, weak people he prefers
To push them like a button door

But he knows the way
And how to reach to a bay
As strategies are chosen in array
And implemented with carrot and stick display
Until everyone conforms without delay

After losing power
Confusion reigns deeper
As the weak person feet order
Can not fit into shoes easier
Of well educated dictator

DR. BELLARIO AHOY NGONG GENG

UNEDUCATED PERSON DISEASE

With power he becomes God incarnate
Not easy to approach under any maneuver
Because he is far hidden from sight
Except through prayers and sacrifices of self
That can be carried out by shoe lickers

Unlike the educated lot
He knows the way not
Making it difficult to reach a goal
There is a difference between what he says
And what he really does

After losing power place
People are relieved so with ease
Joy radiates faces
As future holds promising
Shown by children playing and giggling

PLEA OF ONCE A TYRANT

Oh! People of once my kingdom
Greetings from my heart bottom
How fondly I think of our home
Since to Almighty call I succumbed

Let me pass this message to you over
After meeting the Almighty GOD
What I did while with you brothers and sisters
Was an abuse of HIS ORDER

I became a tyrant
To all HIS laws I was defiant
While HIS order was meant
That I be HIS shepherd

For that he relegated my status
Below each of you fast
And threaten to send me to hell abyss
Unless I apologize to you first

And in return
Request HIM to forgive me as HE worn
Now that I humbly request your learned
Authority to send what I yearn

Otherwise I disappear into gallows
Of everlasting fire glows
All you hear are my whine bellows
And blood gushing out of my eye brows
PLEASE! PLEASE! PLEASE!

RESPONSE OF PEOPLE TO TYRANT PLEA

Oh! Tyrant now you are in your sense
It is too late to repent hence
As repent is possible on earth precincts
And not before the Almighty presence

All what HE offered was not a deal
But was to test our will
Whether we know HIS laws and yield
Or we have forgotten them on a hill

DR. BELLARIO AHOY NGONG GENG

You should have learned more
That all including you on floor
Were born necked and poor
And we go back using the same door

What we acquired on earth
Inform of power and wealth
Is temporary and illusive path
Meant to put target on test

Now that you have failed your test tidy
Do not expect any assistance from us ready
Otherwise we are in the same fate without pity
As you have gone under HIS Almighty

Because HE is testing our will net
As HE has done with you flat
And with Adam and Eve great
Rest assure we shall never do that
NEVER! NEVER! NEVER!

BEHAVIOR OF A WEAK PERSONALITY

When a weak personality sits over
On the wheel of power
Path lay with scent flowers
And lined by loyal bowers

He will only carry lads
Stronger than him on his head
Behaving like a kid
Mincing a tender meat

And will tread upon those under his boots
Slaughter them like goats
Threatening to destroy their roots
Unless they play safe by licking his feet

LOST IN THE FOREST (What can we do?)

To a land of honey and milk, we yearned
Beyond the forest of no return
Nobody knew the meaning of the term
After three weeks walking, we turned
And arrived inside the forest sun-burned

There was no water and food at least
To quench thirst and hunger pains at best
We divided into big groups in the west
Then into small ones in the east
Before being swallowed by the forest

At this juncture we could not proceed
And we could not retreat
Birds sing with voices ridiculing us ahead
While eagles swirled around to rescue our meat
What can we do indeed?

SENIOR HUNTER ADVICE TO A YOUNG HUNTER

Hunting is a good sport
A game meat you can afford
As well as physical fitness support
To extend life before you can depart

But be alert!
For you can get hurt
From wild animals on defense guard
Or from colleagues in disregard

Like politics, if you are on hunting drive
Avoid injuring dangerous animals slight
If you have to injure them to survive
Then do it fatally to save your life

SENSATIONS AND POWER

Without power all the five sensations gears
Of smell, touch, taste, see and hear
Are actively alive with cheers
Any defect must be due to a natural wear

With power icon enabled
See and hear sensations are feeble
A subject can respond to some people
With more power than himself triple

With absolute power
Sensations of smell, touch and taste are stronger
But sensations of see and hear disappear ever
In fact, a subject of absolute power is blind and deaf for ever

COLD WAR *(Defined)*

I'm war, believe me I'm war
But I differ from other wars so far
Because they are open, direct and dire
While I'm indirect, to be noticed is rare
And conduct my warfare by proxy snare

I always follow a major war drain
When parties are fatigued and strained
But still have axes to grind
In that situation I have a shrewd brain
In conducting this business brand

I use so many tactics like water
Because of lack of space here
Some of them will be mentioned later
And some will not appear ever
Because they are my professional matters

COLD WAR TACTICS *(Divide and rule)*

When a master feels his authority is to plop
He will device means to divide a group
And at the same time keep them in a loop
He will encourage small differences to develop
And bitter adversary to crop

Once a leader wanted to achieve his end
By destroying a politically negotiated agreement
He made use of the political rivalry vent

Between the top rival leaders by then
And divided them using tribalism dent

He appointed one to head the battered regions
And the other his vice president
At the end he divided the wagon
Into three acrimonious legions
While he sat in the capital to rule his Nation

COLD WAR TACTICS *(Economic sanction)*

I'm called economic sanction chief
The Powerful use me as a weapon to whip
Those who oppose him until they weep
If they do not surrender cheap

Once a tyrant system having lost totally
The Region politically
Resorted to use me to strangle tightly
The Region economically

Through stopping my trade links
I shall force his adversaries to wing and blink
Until they turn pink
If they do not make him their King

COLD WAR TACTICS *(Job Denial)*

A tribe can target a tribe at a point blank
Or a clique against a clique

To prevent the other group to click
Or stifle the means for honorable life to tick
With an aim of making their future bleak

During a certain war
Deprived people were denied jobs so far
On the ground they had no qualification on gear
And when one presents qualification so rare
He was dubbed to be over radar

When they got people engaged in alcoholic brewing
They would condemn them to prison languishing
And when they fight for a right
They would be declared outlaws marauding
The only way open was a gate of dying

COLD WAR TACTICS (Scapegoat)

Someone is blamed for others' mistakes
Either because the perpetrator is in the deck
Or is powerful and where about is difficult to make
A victim is usually in the line of the perpetrator track
Or carrying the same offensive opinion on the back

In a certain war back, we note
Ordinary citizens were held scapegoats
Under the name of fifth column boat
Some of them were killed on the road
And many languished in prison moats

With the Second World war heated
Jews were slain in gas chambers seated
No Jew Hitler omitted
For mistakes they never committed
Or if committed, it was by few misguided

COLD WAR TACTICS *(Hypocrisy)*

I'm hypocrisy my dear
Cold war use me so far
To deceive his enemies far and near
So that they are caught unaware
For cold war to rid them clear

During the Julius Ceaser's reign
I was living in Brutus' tent
Ceaser's assistant and long time confidant
I caused Brutus to arrange an assassination band
To kill Ceaser and proclaim himself higher on land

Ceaser was assured to stay calm in court
And expected his visitors to come and hail him like god
The visitors became assassins' hordes
With Brutus lodging his fatal knife to finish his lord
You too Brutus! Were Ceaser's last words

COLD WAR TACTICS *(Sabotage)*

They call me saboteur sage
And my job is sabotage

I do this job to serve my political interest
When an enemy is strong to engage
I can exploit its internal weakness to my advantage

During a certain war
Freedom fighters captured me in a car
I was an Officer waging a war against them in that corridor
Because of my ethnic complexion similar to theirs
They placed training of their recruits under my care

I administered harsh conditions since the beginning
To the effect that 50% of recruits perished during my training
Justifying that was to instill endurance rating
I later on boasted to have inflicted a blow to Freedom recruits ring
After I defected back to my place under my original armed wing

CHILDREN OF MY COUNTRY

With Independence in a hall
Do not relax your role
And turn individualistically tall
And pursue personal aims call
Assuming you have achieved your goal

Struggle has many aims
Not less than animals in the game
Diverse and difficult to pitch one name
And complex to the makeup of a nervous system
Than boarding of an independence tram

Although attaining independence
Should first be secured at hands
Unite to fight poverty and ignorance
Before they can unite once
And push you off balance

LEADERS AND THEIR SERVICES

When leaders serve public equally
They serve GOD and posterity
And when they serve individual parity
They serve devil and avarice captivity

Be attentive to what they say first
And match it with their actions blasts
If they say what they do to the nearest
They are serving public interest

But if they say what they do not do so far
They are involved in their individual care
Disentangle yourself from their snare
And mind your own business ware

IF YOU WANT TO BE

If you want to be in a country Z
Whose standards deviate from the normal set
Using strategies that are odd
Underline these tips with red

If you want to rule, acquire physical skills
If you want to be kicked around, in your studies excel
If you want to be rich, combine politics with trading zeal
If you want to have a juicy job, surrender to your mentor will

Do not be a popular giant
Do not acquire skills
Do not be a transparent soul
Do not have respect and integrity seal

PEACE AND WAR

Peace and war are opposite sides of one scale
Each picks up when the other has downed its sails
However peace succeeds
When there had been an intense war wails
And war comes when peaceful means have failed

This is so because while peace delights
In defining the borders between wrong and right
War trims the borders and makes them concrete tight
Rendering them impossible to be penetrated straight
By a stranger unless enjoying a power might

Peace can only prevail when war has exhausted its wits
And when disadvantages of war outweighs its benefits
If you want to keep peace then prepare for war indeed
For war defines the borders of peace to sit
It can then make it to sleep and to snore like a kid

DR. BELLARIO AHOY NGONG GENG

PEOPLE, LEADERS AND WEALTH

Awake!
Open your mind before day break
Then get up from the deck
To understand this paradox in a pack

When wealth hits downturn deeper
People of the target society suffer
As a result of austerity decisions matters
Taken by their leaders

But when fortune lands
Leaders reap the fruits delighted
Even though people have the wealth created
In both situations leaders are not affected

TWO WAYS OF GAINING POWER

Either through loyalty
By winning the mighty
Or through enmity
By bleeding the deity

In one you are a button
Similar to egg but rotten
In the other you are a Titan
Swimming the Gulf of Aden

Better have a brain
That can be trained
Than have a terrain
That can be drained

CHAPTER V

MISCELLANEOUS

INJUSTICE NEVER DIES

It jumps from one party to another like a ghost
Singing its songs in joy and amusement
When it resides in a host
It instructs the host to inject foremost
Its venom into a victim with a toast

When a victim fights back
And the host receives a knock with shock
It will leave the host to its wounds to lick
And wear a winner tag
Causing it to turn its back

It will then attack other victims with vice
And the cycle continues with other guys

In that way injustice never dies
But it goes around like fleas
Knocking one against the other as it flies

JUDICIARY

It is as old as human creation
But still in demand as daily rations
The time it ceases application
Humankind will end its mission

Judiciary mission is to find truth against false
Do not look for truth before sun sails
As it will disappear among mass of owls
That has come at night to measure the court pulse

As truth is heavy
With its weight bearing down on a tummy
The judiciary will be walking bent and weary
As a woman carries on her back a baby

LOOKING FOR MY RIGHT

My right where are you?
You told me to look for you in the battlefield row
When I went there and bow
You left and went to where I don't know

My right where are you?
You then said I find you dividing peace cows
When I approached using the gate below

You disappeared from the other gate at ago
My right where are you?
After completing all searches as police does
A deep voice from nowhere bellowed!
"You will get me inside your grave if you want me true"

EVERY NATION HAS A HEAD, A BODY AND TAIL

Every nation has a head
That plans, direct and leads
Treasures are divided in order of descend
The nearest getting the teat
And the furthest to curl in wait

It also has a body
A factory of goodies
To be distributed solely
By the head to the needy
The remnants given to a naughty

It has a tail
That wags on head happiness
And sings between legs when the head wails
Being malnourished, it is thin and pale like criminal in jail
The first to sleep and the first to wake up on call

MOUNTAIN ON MY ROAD

I used to tread that road
It was smooth and straight by God
That passes through green land wood

Nothing was on the way to note
At a sudden with no warning
When I was back from the journey
One fateful early morning
I found a mountain on my road anchoring

I stood in awe
Bewildered and stunned like a Jew
A bright apparition broke into view
Telling me to wait for suffering days will be few

PRISON

I'm not home
For I do not provide a mattress foam
And I do not allow adult to stay with mom
As they used to do so when they were at her womb

I'm not a bush
Where there hide beasts with ugly teeth
Observing every movement in a watch
And biting at unripe fruits to have their hunger pains soothed

I'm in between
As it is not a place for gain
But a place to lean
When one has committed a sin

REAL FREEDOM

Freedom comes from toil
To secure it all
You have to till a soil
Until you get it submerged in oil

Freedom comes from sweat
When you work up the heartbeat
As a result of body heat
You get it by reaping wheat

Freedom comes from self reliance
Defend on your produce including wild
Treat everything given free with defiance
And there it comes in company of King Lion

AT LAST CROCODILE IS MADE A CHIEF

He pleaded for a Hippo King
Of rivers to make him a chief
Of Deep Hole colony
The king declined knowing his short comings
Including the fact that he would reduce without a blink
The colony population to virtual extinct
Noting his greedy and gluttonous craving

But he enticed, kissed, licked and flapped
At last the king gave in and was made chief the beloved
All inhabitants of the Hole attended the ceremony in the club
Some wonder as they know his nature

Whether or not he would knock them with a club
And turn them into food stuff
Others think he has changed and gave him a cheering clap

In one year the population of fishes was reduced into half
All living things distanced themselves from him
Except little birds whose function is to pick meat pulps
Lodged among the teeth gaps
They have to be careful not to hit on the chief nerves
Otherwise they are swept in with gigantic tongue wave
And consumed as well in the same style of wolves

HOW WOLF BECAME A SHEPHERD

Fools!
They are ardent fools
How do they make a wolf in sheep wool
Shepherd for the livestock pools
Now it is feeding on bulls
Next time it will consume them all

Listen and understand lad
Do not pass a judgment yet
There was a situational threat
That made it possibly of late
For a wolf head
To be crowned a shepherd

A great misfortune descended on a village
Without delay cattle, goats and sheep met carnage
Disappearing at a rate that has no match

At last children were the next batch
Village folks hunted beast for revenge
But it was devouring them as if they were cakes

Like Mena falling from the sky
A herd of wolves came on hunting spree
Their eyes fell on a beast devouring a donkey
In a short time there was no any
As they tore it into pieces without delay
And devoured it, nothing left to decay

Human kind being regardful
Was then grateful
And selected from wolves' herd
A chief wolf as a shepherd to rule
As it liberated them in full
From the fangs of a lion so powerful

Is it so Daddy?
Oh! Poor humans in tragedy
They escape one danger so deadly
To run into another so ghastly
More pernicious as it acts so lethally
Do they have a remedy?

SELF IMPOSED VIGILANTE

This is my area nicknamed free zone
The soil of my birth alone
Any one tempering with its stone
Will bear my rage inform of fire balls

My group and I naturally seasoned
Are in charge of areas including towns
With its people bending their heads down
Never to see where their Properties have gone

And when all threats are over
I need to satisfy my appetite
Anything of value must come to me
Money livestock and beautiful wives
Never question my desire drive
Otherwise you bear my wrath
This can be inform of destroying your tribe
Your wealth, your family and if need be your life

I do not fear all men
Any one that crosses my land
Even God knows my intent
One time he wanted me a Saint
To respect the Ten Commandments
But I violated all at the end
Except the first four
Because they don't worth value of a pen

THE BEST WE HAVE

Although they extend to me a hand
Full of Rands
And when I receive it to meet my wants
They withdraw and put it in their under pants
And drove away in a van
Endure; this is the best we have

Although I need good governance
Conducting business with transparency
And appointing people on merits quality
But you see people appointed on personal loyalty
And on the bases of give and take boldly
Endure; this is the best we have

I desire prosperity clicking
So that I enjoy fruits reaping
To make the periods of upheavals disappearing
But I'm not getting
Because the treasury bag is leaking
Still endure; this is the best we have

THIEVES IN A SYSTEM

Nonsense! Don't and never believe
I'm not a thief
What I have taken chief
Was advanced as a gift
A pay for public money I kept
I swear that was not a strip
Taken from an individual rib

How can I be branded thief? By a clique
Thieves steal individual properties
While this action is bonus for hard work I did
A work I rendered to public
If I do not pay myself, who else would pay me
Public cannot do so
Because they can't own even a brick

Moreover by right of precedence
I saw my boss paying himself in tens
Quite a good sum for prominence
Who I'm with cents and pence
To resist jumping over a fence
Only a fool cannot dance
When climbing a ladder of affluence

MEAT AND HUNGRY DOGS

Once there was a game hunting on the move
But animals were rare, never found in groups
When the team was almost losing hope
After two days hunting without stop
Dogs spotted the antelope

They ran as their legs could carry them
After killing and meat has been prepared by name
The hunters gave dogs their shares to take home
As they were very tired to walk as fast as they came

The pieces of meat were packed
And hanged around the dogs' necks
Dangling from side to side as they went back
The whole scenario was a tempting act
All dogs helped themselves with their packs

Never give responsibility to hungry lots
Those are hungry both in their bellies and hearts
They will suck you dry by lord!
Leaving you groaning with pain of regret

FIGHTING WITH A LION

Hours and hours he fought the lion alone
No one came from direction of his town
And no one came thrown
From the opposite direction by cyclone
The lion was fierce, agile and wearing a golden crown
And so is the young man standing out among millions

After receiving many painful hits from the man
The lion left to a distance to rest stunned
The man thought it gave up the fight
And foolhardily threw away his magic club at his hand

On seeing this, lion came back like tiger
And attacked the young man with vigor
Whereby his fate was sealed with resistance meager
Foolish is a person who under rates his enemy ever
Even if the enemy plays a game of surrender

INSECTS PICKED THE GAUNLET

He thinks insects are weak without power
When sprayed they easily die in millions more
But when he met with a division of *muor muor**
He forgot pigs were filthy poor
And embrace them to rescue him sure

He said his faith is great like python
And brandish his weapon
But when he met with battalions of scorpions

He thought his faith was a vision
And ran towards the north direction

He thought insects were cowards to the brim
But when swarms of bees ambushed him
Stinging every area of his skin rim
He dropped the keys of his paradise at whim
But bees picked them and gave him to secure his dream
*little ants

GUEST HAS GROWN HORNS

He came wearing a gaunt face and a gloomy mood
The face bitten by sandstorm he met when en route
And wearing a cloak of his faith strewn with jute
With prayer beads in his hand as he stood
Asking for shelter, water and food

When he had all these graced
And was now wearing a lively face
He praised god of his faith
Made the host kneel underneath
And to close both eyes to praise

By which he took host land
Shelter and women
As for men
He wanted them without mind
Or as slave eunuchs in Aden

He praised again the god his king
And arranged a feast of thanks giving
By which he promised not to sin under HIS watching
And in response to his pleading
God gave him keys for heaven lodge

PATRIOTISM

Patriotism is when you yourself agree
To sacrifice with sweat, blood and soul free
To liberate or response to your country plea
Going barefooted and sleeping under shadow trees

Patriotism is when struggle is all over cleared
You stay idle or hide yourself below the grave yard
Leaving others to enjoy the fruits of struggle mart
And praising you for the job well done at start

Patriotism is when some of colleagues mindless
Tend to be more equal while considering others hopeless
Because of their role in showing them in fullness
How to fight, eat and pee in the wilderness

HIGH POPULARITY (I)

Fellow of senior generation
You one who commands my admiration
I envy those who are popular in all nations
When they approach the congregation
People stand up in ovation

And when they laugh in animation
People laugh in unison
I want to be highly popular in my station
How do I make it to my satisfaction?

Fellow of junior generation of my city
There are two ways of making popularity
Either you are extremely good and full of generosity
Or extremely bad and clad with barbarity
Both are respected and adored for curiosity
Respect and adoration for good deeds is gentility
While respect for bad deeds though in rarity
Is either an appeasement from aggrieved party
Or genuine for those who fish out of calamity

Since one can be popularly praised
In any of both ways
Does it pay?
If one takes
Any of the ways with ease
What are the pros each way obeys?
And cons each way portrays?
I want an easy case
With short cut to popularity bays

HIGH POPULARITY (II)

I advise you to choose the good way twice
Provided that you must be so nice
A rare personality like prophets of Christ
Choosing this approach needs self sacrifice

That includes self denial thrice
You may also lose your life as a price
While engaging in good and generosity ties
But the good part in this Mr. Wise
Is you secure heaven before those guys

In case you chose the bad way approach
You must be as cruel as a beast in a bush
And secure in a rush
Your demise quickly with a splash
And way to hell later with a crash
Unless you cover your deeds so much
By constantly praying and lighting a torch
In the Almighty church
To have your sins washed

Come near and bring your ears close my friend
So that I can whisper this to them as you bend
"Some people are using this tactic any way in their dens"
They take God for granted making use of the teaching sent
"You will be forgiven if you repent"
And because HE does not punish people instant
Try this way on your own accord gentleman
And do not take it as my advice behind a curtain
As I have washed my hand thoroughly with a detergent

EQUALITY BEFORE LAW

There is one thing I know
And I can take a vow
I know it well as my toe

DR. BELLARIO AHOY NGONG GENG

For five years I learned it sure and slow
In the school of law

Law is great and sparkling
It is so high and towering
That no one is above its level
All people are below and bowing
In reverence when he approaches beaming

Do not be naïve
It is true law without bribe
Is great, tall and sharp
But some people strive
To be taller than the law drive

I tell you something dear
You do not know clear
I acquire this knowledge my friend
Through my long years
Of experience practicing law sphere

Power when acquired by some people
They turn the law feeble and cripple
With iron fist they can break it double
Once I held the law high up like golden apple
And what happened while I grappled?

Some people as giants gathered
And as all elephants put together
Broke it into pieces like a feather
I tried to rush it to the hospital theatre
But with no avail it passed away later

COURTS AND THEIR LIMITS (I)

So happy, happy, so happy
So secure, secure in a canopy
So free, free from past so murky
So glad, glad like a child entertained with lullaby
So proud, proud like a soldier wearing khaki
So lucky, lucky to get a carbon copy
So peaceful, peaceful after getting a right therapy

What gives you high spirit my friend in struggle?
Trust me I'm alone single
So that I fly with you in company of eagles
To pass over the jungles
As we giggle
On our way to Los Angeles
Where everything we touch is regal

I'm damn free and secure
Our courts system can handle with maturity
All cases with decor
Starting from local to high without demur
They are straight forward and pure
The injustice how small they take care
Never allow intimidation or corruption to obscure

COURTS AND THEIR LIMITS (II)

I beg your pardon; you are in all accounts unwary
Did you say they are not to be intimidated really?
I'm sorry you must be living in heaven sanctuary

And watching earth with parochial spectacles you carry
As far as I know courts can handle cases fairly
With ease and competence necessary
When they are few, less severe and from people ordinary

As for cases that
Deluge the system flat
Or very severe involving lot of people dead
Or those holders of master cards
And the holders of power jets
They shy away like rats
Encountering cats

Ah! There is a grain of truth in practice
But I beg you not to spoil my day at least
You see he has closed a door of his office!
I was singing and dancing to Lord Justice
To give me something for my breakfast with ease
Now he has closed the door as if shutting out a beast
I beg if you can compensate with a pound as I have missed

IF SUSPECTED THIEVES QUARREL THE REAL THIEF WILL BE FOUND

Have you heard news Jack?
What news my friend I beg?
The squanderers were caught and sacked
How were they found in fact?
While they say they are elusive full of tact
Quite difficult to stick out their necks
To be identified intact

They quarreled aloud
One accused the others in a shout
To have taken more than allowed
And so they ended exchanging bitter words
Accusing each other in the crowd
And the real thieves hiding out
Were found and identified in the wood

That is great my friend in deed
And so what will happen next ahead?
They will be forced in a bit
To return the property
And to be prosecuted of greed
Before the court of law with speed
Since for the law no one is above its limit

That is fantastic!
That means if you want to go out
And catch a thief among thieves so elusive
Then cause them to quarrel
And the real thief will appear like ballistic missile
Thank you for great lesson so classic
I have learned today in a way so dramatic

JUDGES ARE ALSO HUMAN

Institution of judges, deserves my salute
For everyone aggrieved gets his toil
Without them injustices prevail
As everyone does at will
World will be in turmoil
And anarchy will reign without recoil

No my dear! You are in a cage
By overstating their status at large
And magnifying their image
Don't you know that they wear a human tag?
And that they have relatives to page
And their special needs to gauge

I advise you child
To reserve that praise sealed
For a person who is deaf still
Blind and does not eat or feel
That person is enjoying real
Eternal life under Almighty zeal

ESCAPING TOWARDS EAST

All directions were closed except the east
After the dice was cast
Young people moved at last
Leaving their home to unwelcome guest

The year was 1983
People moved in a hurry
Only to rest under big trees
Their goal was yearning to be free

Welcome from the east was warm
The situation was calm
And young people got training and arms
To return back strong and firm

PANTHOU

When thunderbolt hit my house plot
My children scattered like flood
And as a result they wandered away in the wood
After much struggle with sweat and blood
I found most of them in a straw with broken mood

But others including Panthou
My first born was not found in a straw
At last I heard of her when put on a show
She was chained and placed in a dungeon below

After a long time of twenty years
She was made a slave to cut her masters' hairs
And doing all the maiden chores in tears
But most importantly unlike her peers
She was vomiting black gold to their cheers

I was angry and devastated by crime
I visited her for ten days prime
And managed to release her with triumph
To breathe the air of freedom for the first time

But alas! The captors ran to elephants reporting danger
And complaining I was a stranger
Abducting their daughter
Mindlessly I was ordered to leave her again to her captors
What justice is that? Do elephants dispense justice?

DR. BELLARIO AHOY NGONG GENG

WHY ARE THEY HARSH ON ME ALONE?

By force he took my land
I complained and rant
And all ears were deaf
And all eyes were blind

He came back to attack me
I complained across seas
And no one heard my plea
And no one saw my land to be

When I retaliated the third time
Dogs barked, bulls bellowed and monkeys giggle
Even if I did not make any trespass with my sickle
Why are they not able to see? Do they need eyes of eagles?

HE CAME BACK AGAIN AND GAVE A FATAL BLOW

I ambushed them among trees
Subdue them with ease
And capture them like bees
Branding them status of POWs

But through my humane heart I released them
They went back to the front line like storm
Their nationalism flowing like a stream
And delivered a pernicious attack just the same

They surrounded and captured me before I realized
That these were POWS released in disguise

They spat this advice to me "You civilian soldier rise!
Go and study war tactics thrice"

CHILD IS WEANED FOR ANOTHER TO COME

Some rulers stay in power for long like a tomb
Even if they are weak and incapacitated at home
They do not want to give others room
Not remembering the fact that with Mom
Child is weaned for another to come

Some stay in a post until doom
And when they are relieved to make way to some
They resist to a point of beating a war drum
Not remembering the wisdom that at home
Child is weaned for another to come

Some keep sucking honey comb
And when asked to give chance to Tom
They protest with cluster bombs
Not remembering the stark wisdom
That a child is weaned for another to come

CHILD ONCE BORN CANNOT BE RETURNED TO A WOMB

Even if we are on rightfulness
Still you declared enmity against us mindless
In addition you have the temerity nevertheless
To treat our Independence as baseless
As if you gave us through your own kindness

By God!
We shall never release an inch to your throat
Of our territory to satisfy your ambitious plot
As we vow not to take a dot
From anyone's territorial slot

Already you were pregnant with doom
You had a painful labor that would have sent you to a tomb
Until doctors were called to deliver you prompt
Yet you want us to return to your bosom
 No Sir, child once born cannot be returned to a womb

INFORMATION

Information is a double edged sword
On one edge it is useful a lot
And can lift human progress forward
When the odds are pointing downwards

On the other edge
It may cause anger and rage
Especially when it is about people in power
Even if the truth is real as proved by a judge

The sources for information face a dilemma real
If they expose the truth, they face a jail
And if to the pressure they yield
They may risk losing credibility zeal

REPENT AND YOU WILL BE FORGIVEN

There are people with hearts hardened
Those who misunderstand the scriptures written
They keep repenting when they are rotten
In order to be forgiven often

They avoid facts without doubt
Those which are clear and loud
Only mistakes committed blunt
Can be forgiven once on note

Mistakes committed quite often
With a hope of repent
Is like throwing a hen in a fox den
With a hope to return

KINDS OF PRISONS

In our search for what kind of prisons are here
We found one for criminals there
Where those who have committed crimes are kept under swear
After they have been sentenced by courts fair

Passing along we found another
Where economy keeps its victims together
Their crime they have not worked harder
For a job that is not there
And they have not stolen from public fund

Going along is another where crew keeps its captain
They protect him from knowing peoples' reaction
To his leadership direction
The difference with the first two prison corrections
Is that the captain is not aware he is in prison

KNOWLEDGE

You are the most precious possession
Human beings have on concession
From GOD discretion
When HE made HIS creation

With your power the humans control creatures
Even the ones more dangerous
Elevating the human greatest
In what GOD has made precious

You remain virtuous forever
Light for the secret of our keeper
As we move hither and thither
Across the river

PART II

CHAPTER II

RELATIONS AND BEHAVIOR

THE ASSASSINS OF A KING LION

Every time there is meal from a prey
Hunted and provided by a pride
The King Lion and lieutenants devour it dry
Leaving the pride to lick the tray

A congregation was arranged by a lion kind
They prayed for Almighty to shine
And gives power to young nine
To free them from the giant

A voice interrupted from the sky
Your prayers are well received in a dairy
But do not subject young to danger unnecessarily
Lieutenants themselves will kill the King out of a folly

THERE IS ONLY A RARE CHANCE TO SLAP A KING

King is an icon of power
And the most powerful ever
When the powerful reigns higher
No one can come nearer
Unless you bow lower

Even that no one touches skin
Except those on the bed lying
And the feet licking
To keep Majesty comfortable
While others are reduced to begging

However there is an occasion rare
When those who care
Can approach the King nearer
And slap the cheek harder
It is when a fly on his cheek retires

RICH AND POOR

There is no rich and poor
Management makes the difference wide
Good management creates riches more

While poor management like war
Turns poverty worst
Many wait for capital to create wealth
Reality is that they will wait until death
Capital as small as your body health
Invested toiling the soil of the earth
Can create it to your girth

Do not wait any longer my dear
Shake out your intense fear
And pick up your mighty oar
After positioning the light gear
You must row towards riches this year

DIALOGUE WITH A SELFISH, GREEDY PERSON
(Dialogue between Mr. Waiting Luck and Mr. Ambition)

Mr. Waiting Luck:
"Can you give me a piece of our cake?
Which together we baked
For our need sake
Last night I was hunger awake
My belly throughout ached"

Mr. Ambition:
"I shall not give you
This cake my family saw
Give me your hoe
And to your home you go"

Mr. Waiting Luck:

"How can you refuse me my cake and add my hoe on the top?
As there is no hope
Give me a rope
To hang myself up
In this world, I can't cope"

Mr. Ambition:
"Ha! Ha! Mr. Waiting Luck
Go to the river bank
And bring to me that lame duck
And continue to wait for your luck
Otherwise kiss a soil and suck"

A LIAR WHO SAVED A MAN'S LIFE

A man killed his rival
He then ran away for his survival
To the direction of the liar behind a temple
People ran after to revenge evil with evil

The man approached the liar
And pleaded to be hidden under
Since he is tired
From running, escaping danger

The liar beckoned him to an open hole
Surrounded only with poles
Straight and tall
And strong enough not to fall

When the revenge team inquired
The liar showed them the real hole required

But the team did not believe him square
Dismissed to be delaying them for a culprit to escape faster
Thus a man was saved by the liar saying the truth the first time ever

EFFECT OF HATRED

When you prevail
You are dangerous and fatal
Mowing a lot of people down in a battle
The destruction left is total

A tool for end justifies the means
When you are followed by ugly scenes
And all fall dead including teens
With bodies spread around like beans

Your disadvantages are for many
Those who have lost their honey
In a situation canny
Premeditated by money

Your advantages are for few
Those who sit in a front pew
With temerity to chew and swallow
What has been vomited by you

WHEN RIGHTS MIX UP WITH WRONG

Mix up is right and wrong
When one is to hang

Because of his tongue
And when one a mute monk
Is forced to sing a song

Mix up is right and wrong
When one points to a moon
And say it is a sun
 And when one picks a phone
And say it is a bone

Mix up is right and wrong
When one talks of equality
But that can only apply in a city
And when one describes horrible scenery
But without pity

PEOPLE OF LIMITED ASSISTANCE

To people of limited assistance
Do not tell your problems in advance
Even if they are fans
Cheering you up with dance

Because they panic on hearing a gong
They either increase them by solutions wrong
Or desert you so far long
To play alone your own ping pong

In both cases you lose
As you will be like a mouse
Falling into a hot sauce
To escape cat paws

BEWARE OF HYPOCRITES

When successful they shower you plentiful
With flowers and praises up to the fill
Facing down humbled to your soul
They exact as they want to the full

But when you are in difficulties
They jump away like fleas
Leaving you on your knees
With frogs to kiss

On being the bosses
They never response to your praises
Even when you wipe their feet with roses
For they wear steel hearts that cannot be softened by Moses

EVERYONE HAS A HUMAN OBSTACLE/PROMOTER IN LIFE

Everyone has a human obstacle in life
That prevents one from achieving delight
Some are justified on competition drive
Others are baseless with selfish pride

And everyone has a human promoter in life
That makes one to rise to higher echelons with a knife
Some are made with potential interests to ripe
And others are purely to keep humanitarianism alive

Never get worry when you get obstacles
For a solution patience and time are critical

And never take for granted your promoter
They need a little praise from you as you settle

LANDS LODGED COMPLAINTS

He reported to an office near the river
With a stuffy face as if covered with paper
His mind was still heavy so ever
 With the liquor hangover
For alcohol, he is a boozer

He was still in his semi stupor descent
When lands complaining of mistreatments
Stormed the office tent
The officer inquired about what was so urgent
As this was an unusual event

All lands in chorus voices so hoarser
Complained of their ill treatments noisier
Masters exchanged hands over them as if playing with feathers
One day with one the other day with another
They felt tired going from one hand to the other

They needed a respite documented bearing his initials
"Go away with your filthy complaints" said the official
"If you don't change from one hand to another like diesel
 I would not be in state I'm enjoying now special"
He confirmed that decision to be final

BEHAVIOR OF RICHES

I'm Riches, the controller of life gears
I caused people to behave queer
When I climb up the stairs
My subject change all belongings at my rear
And acquire those with higher value with cheers

When I come down the ladder
My subject change all belongings under
Those glittering wonders
And acquire tatters
With lower value faster

Under my influence acting
Undesirable friendship standing
Breaks up crashing
As nothing is permanent and existing
When I'm in the helm directing

RIGHTEOUS PATH VERSUS CROOKED PATH (I)

Why do you stand at cross roads?
Seemingly confused with thoughts?
Oh young man wearing a coat!
If you cannot proceed with your load
Can you either retrace steps of your feet?
Or find a shelter near your spot
Take; here is an umbrella and a sandwich of food

I'm bewildered on what way I take
Ahead of me are two roads at stake
One is straight and smooth like a snake
I'm tempted to follow it to try my luck
But I see a head bumps and swinging bridges as they shake
I'm afraid I may fall on my back
Get drown or break my neck

Another road is crooked with sharp turns
 With official flags studding the roads without end
I wonder what is the government concern
Shall I not get into trouble at every bend?
Making the whole scenario more confused gentlemen
Is the presence of a link path as it runs
Between the righteous and crooked lanes

RIGHTEOUS PATH VERSUS CROOKED PATH (II)

I see what!
You are really young and inexperienced lad
Both roads are given names by the Almighty God
The straight one is called righteous slot
 And the zigzag one is called crooked b-road
All are linked by a path so that one can move like a rat
 From one path to the other depending on availability of bread

The righteous has bumps and swinging bridges
If not careful it can break your neck to pieces
Or get drowned to be food for fishes
Only the few righteous that can persevere over ages
Can continue to heaven as sages

The crooked one has government laws placed on its sides
To prevent it from dragging many to hell ditches

Yet there are few I can tell
Who could go and kneel
Through the laws grid but enter hell
For what to do is a matter of personal will
Either to end up in heaven or to hell malt
However there is opportunity to revert as well
To either of the roads if you are good at a drill

BANKING DILEMMA (I)

Situation has changed fast
In the past
When one is in a banking task
Details are kept close to the chest
Secret and confidential at best
No other person is admitted to pass
Even the most trustworthy host

Good that you are aware
Now banking anywhere
Has no security care
And to make matters weird
These days one must lay bare
The source of money ware
And how one has acquired it fair

My God of creation!
They want to know in precision

Whether money has a terrorists' connection
Or stolen from countries trodden upon by corruption
But what about a person
Banking billions earned alone
Through sweat and toil by breaking stones?

BANKING DILLEMMA (II)

Still they want to know in earnest
The duration of acquiring wealth
If short, you are suspect from birth
If long, you are honorable with health
Yet one still produces proof of work beneath
That proof can only be provided after death
When judgment is handed down to earth

Stop these long hours
Of useless seminars
Since space exploration among stars
Has reached its zenith far
What if one banks so far
On another planet such as mars
And avoid these inconveniences so dire?

Oh! Yes, Mars made of stones red and brown
But Mars is so far away to be habited soon
It is possible to bank on what we own
Near here on the moon
Provided that before going to the zone
One takes permission by phone
From Mr. Ban Ki-moon

JOBLESS

A person with no work to earn a living is jobless
Another name to crown him is a title powerless
To the employer ears his pleadings are baseless
At the end he finds solace in idleness
As he stays jobless and nervous
His life is joy less

Longer without, he will be hopeless
To public interest
He will care less
More time still he will be lawless
Without remedy he attends criminal classes
On the way to a pit fathomless

If you want to be blessed
And appear the tallest
Even though you are short nonetheless
Acquire rare skills in earnest
To avoid remaining jobless

BEHIND THE SMILING FACES

Behind the smiling faces is hypocrisy
It lives in a darken abode called jealousy
As it feeds on information brought by hearsay
It delivers its policy devoid of mercy

This is their favorable dress
Made of crafted interwoven grass

In the compound full of trees
They sat to address the press

Hidden under is a sinister lot
Placed in an awful pot
Is it made of what?
You can tell not

If you open and get caught
You will get it hot
Better leave it to rot
Before eroding your foot

WALKING PROUDLY

One has a proudly walk
When life smiles on the face with luck
Giving several embraces of hugs
And lifting one off the yoke

The blood in a system rises
Giving a mighty walk in phases
The first being heavier than last touches
In all around, one distributes happy teases

If you are a humane person, look inquisitively down
You might be stepping on other people toes with tons
For it is by tramping on other peoples bones
That propels one to walk proudly as if on the moon

CATCHING A THIEF

Catching a thief on your own
That is a matter marooned
With life and death around
Be ready to carry arrest warrant
From the prosecutor desk
In addition, you should be on moral high ground
To undertake that mission sound

You should not be standing thither
Colluding with thieves hither
And at the same time want to catch others
You should be stronger than a thief wizard
In all accounts of physical power
And should never at any time ever
Alert a thief to sense a campaign fever

Otherwise thieves are so canny and elusive
They will knock one down dead stiff
Before one catches them conclusive
And they will never vomit
Anything they have swallowed before
Even if their heads are turned over leaf
And tapping made hard on their back four times five

ESSENCE OF GOOD RELATIONS

Some people when assisted
Gets away with it without appreciation
And never mind the return of services

Even when they are in a position to do so
They feel degraded to express
The support given to them
Not only that but some has the temerity
To return the good with evil
To extent of remorselessly
Hurting the supporter

This makes some people withhold support
They can offer to others
The result, that society goes down the drain
 Without progress and development

Lucky is that society
When their members receive support
From each other give appreciation
And return of services in abundance
In that way they will encourage
More support and assistance
And the society goes up
The ladder of development
In peace, love and harmony
How happy they will be

WHAT IS AT STAKE

They search and get on board
Anything glittering like gold
And anything smooth like sponge
More still on board
Is anything that makes them enjoy time
Or quench their intensive thirst

In the main they look
At one side of the coin only
They do not examine the object
On its sideways
Or at its bottom or thickness
Or its background

They do this not knowing that
It is not knowing what you want
Which is at stake
But of not knowing
Where and how to find
What you want

NO PLACE FOR TENDER HEART IN THE WORLD

Disheartened and disappointed
Tender heart knocked hard
The door of the Almighty
Conveying his complaint
He delivered it in a revered
And humble tone

When created
The Almighty assigned him
To the world to sooth hearts
And to lubricate peace joints
But when he arrived
Things fell apart

At times of peace
Cowards and Opportunists reign
They do not need tender heart
As he will prevent them
To loot and enrich themselves
Before war relieves them of their duties

During war times
The brave and greedy enjoy
They do not need tender heart
As it will prevent them
From messing quick wealth
Before peace curtails their fortunes

The Almighty having listened
And understood the complaint
Told tender heart
To wait until the Day of Judgment of the World
As he is very busy judging the other bodies
Those like the world have ended their lives in the universe!

TIME CAN BE A SOLUTION

When available options
To a solution of a problem
Are not desirable
Do not lose hope
Time waited with patience
Can bring solution
To your surprise

As you wait
Certain options will be outdated
And fail the test of time
Others lose the appeal
And one option will definitely shine
Or presents itself as a better evil
Among all evils

And so what, if time cannot offer a solution
As one may suddenly die
Cutting off the time and patience
Even with that, never mind
As time will follow you to the grave
And rise with you, the time of judgment
Only the sacrilegious will not understand this

TRUTH AND FALSE AT A BALANCE

One is at a fix to judge
A case between two people
One has a right
But with no power support behind
The other is wrong but with power behind

Due to negative consequences inherent
In the judgment of truth against a powerful false case
Avoid being a judge in such a situation
But if you have to
Better uphold the former

For you can lose a fight
And win a war
Rather than win a fight
And lose a war
When you uphold the latter

TO BE HATED FOR NOTHING

Who says I'm hated
For something bad I do
If I do bad things
That is obvious
But I can also be hated
For something I have not done
And worst still I can be hated
By people I had supported or rescued
From sliding with mud down the hill

That sounds grim indeed
What then can one do?
To avoid being hated
Nothing
But it is better to be hated while innocent
Than to be hated for bad things you do
For the former you have clear conscience
As for the latter you have sick conscience
Even if you pretend to be normal

IN SEARCH OF GOOD

Good is not cheap
If it was, everyone will acquire it
In the process it loses its value
And will never be good again

Good is very expensive
Not everyone can afford to get it
To acquire it, you must be intelligent
 A rich person or both

Good does not exist in huge quantities
And never found in the neighborhood
If it was so available and so near
Everyone will own it

Good is rare and stays far away
Where you exert
Efforts to obtain it
After sweating and exhaustion

Heed the wise sayings
That has passed the tests of times
Oh, Maker of Events!
Do not pick anything that glitters
Assuming that it is good
"For all that glitters is not gold"
It may be a skin of a snake
Glittering on moon light!

DR. BELLARIO AHOY NGONG GENG

STEPPING ON FEET OF INTENSE HATRED

He hates me!
By God, he hates me!
It is a burning hate
So hot that water
And sand can't extinguish it
That hate was falling on an innocent target
For I was not aware of it

But he never said a word
Or revealed to someone else his motives
He only uses his body sign, posture and omission
To send his lethal message to me
I could see the furnace inside him
Through his eyes moving in haste
Like a molten rock from the volcano outburst

It was at a distance of five feet that I saw it
Slowly I traced and traced my feet back
Until I moved away from his sight
But he still follows me
Not with his eyes but with his long tentacles
Is he an octopus?
Only the Creator can save my soul

RESPECT

You want to be respected?
Do not fight for it
Do not force others unto it

But look inward
Do first what can attract respect
And you will get respect in abundance
On a golden plate

But what are the things
That command respect?
You mean you do not know?
Don't you remember?
The teachings of CHRIST
Come on let us recapture
"Do to others what you would like them to do to you"

This is complicated
What is it in simple expression?
It means as you like to be treated fairly
Treat others fairly first
From there you gain
The respect of every body
From the bottom of their hearts

But this is a farfetched virtue
It can be reached by those
Who are taller in faith than I?
As for me I'm a dwarf in faith
And a myopic in vision
What I can reach and see is the physical force
Which I like to use to keep people in line behind me

DR. BELLARIO AHOY NGONG GENG

WHY DO I BEHAVE LIKE THAT?

Why do I behave like that?
As if no one can do the work
And as if the world is stupid and unable
Depending on me alone

Don't I know this?
I'm really ignorant
For I think I'm the only one
Nonsense, there are those
Even better than me
They are there before
And they will be there tomorrow

Still I live in the cage of illusion
Indulge in inferiority and mediocrity
Losing all my senses except appetite
Never allow it to unfurl!
For I have a long sticky tongue
That can sweep in all that is juicy and delicious
Leaving you to lick the empty dishes at the end

BY GOD, I HAVE BEEN TAKEN FOR A RIDE

This is non sensible, I'm frustrated
I use to believe you're a good teacher
From now I shall not believe
A single word from you
How can you teach that
When there is darkness the stars will shine
I'm now in darkness and I do not see stars shinning

Sorry, what I did not tell you is this
You see the stars
When you are in darkness below the stars
But when one is in deep darkness beyond the stars
You will not see any star again
There, is the outside space quite serene
And leading to infinity

Once you are there you will be in darkness
Until thy Kingdom come
Either you are released to a new light
A place with ground made of honey and milk
Or you will be condemned to a land of abysmal stretch
Have I made a sense out of this subject?
Yes sir, it is clear like a sunny day

WAY TO GOOD LIFE

The professor tried hard and harder
He prepared his lessons carefully and meticulously
To convince a student adamant
To climb his way up to life paradise

That life must be traced
Through a straight line devoid of evil
Especially as others are concerned
Never hurry or bulldoze your way
While leaving others groaning with tears

He showed him many ways to reach the life worth
The best is to go on straight line up to the end

The average is to start straight but go zigzag towards the end
The worst is to start zigzag and continue towards the end

But adamant as he is
He chose the last option
Because to him
Life is here
He does not believe in life after death

POWER AND TIMIDITY LEADS TO DISASTER

I came to a generation who is not mine
And came to a city I'm not welcome
And join a struggle I'm not needed
And take a meal I'm not invited
Love someone who does not love me
Helped someone who hates me

But how come you sing that gloomy song?
Are you disappointed, dispirited and forlorn?
Come on let us sing a hopeful song
Provided that you shun your intelligence and follow me
To serve under a giant so powerful but timid
He commands and bulldozes without direction

Wait a bit; this is so serious and dangerous
How can I serve under a person without direction?
And swim in an ocean without end?
And also a person so timid
Don't you know that power plus timidity leads to disaster?
Only the naive will not comprehend that fact

TALKING TO A PERSON WITH WEIRD SENSIBILITY

I see a monster with long ears
Its claws that of a beast
But he sees a handsome lad full of charm
He longs for his company

I hear a person with horse voice
Words flow incongruously
But he hears him with sweet voice
His voice mimics that of a dove

I smell an odor
So sickening and nauseating
But he smells the same so tantalizing
He keeps his nose on course

I tasted food she brought weird
To force it would trigger a vomit
But she tasted it so delicious
Saliva flows uncontrollably

I touch the skin so rough and tingling
Its continuity invites excruciating pain
But he touches it so smooth and comfortable
Its essence nourishes soul

I think of future being dark and bleak
As drivers are unfaithful and corrupt
But he courts the thoughts of bright future
As he sees people honest and transparent

DR. BELLARIO AHOY NGONG GENG

THOSE WHOSE BEHAVIORS MATCH

They move and stick together like feathers
They meet, strategize and put into action
Leaving you out in a cold
Kicking your heels
And you have to wonder why you are left out
Not knowing that those who work together
Are those whose thinking and behavior match

When they need privacy
They go to the secret place
Organize their affairs in the morning
And in the evening they go for a walk on the river side
And you become surprised why you have been left out
Not knowing that those who walk together
Are those whose thinking and behavior match

They leave you here; fly to the island of moon
Away from the noises of the earth
To spend a holiday full of ecstasy
Before they return back
And you bitterly complain that you have been left out
Not knowing that those who stay together
Are those whose thinking and behavior match

LOOKING FOR GOOD

Why do you move forward and backward?
Right and left
What do you want?

Are you looking for good?
But why are you hesitant to take decision?
Do you think you can get it without price to pay?

No my dear
Come on
If you do not know
Then keep alert all your senses
And discern this

Good needs sacrifice
Especially those that affect one personal interest
As for bad you do not need sacrifice at all
It just comes by omission of not doing good

ARGUMENT BETWEEN AN OPTIMIST AND A PESSIMIST

They argue and argue and argue
An optimist said a day is always bright
Even at night
Provided that one prepares
Provisions that make it glitters
Whatever blocks the way
Is the means to gain success

A pessimist said a day is always dark
Whatever one prepares
It is always dark and gloomy
During the day one is disturbed
By strange noises of creatures
And at night it is so silent
With stars blinking threateningly

A day is never dark or bright
It is one who makes it the other way

OPERATING BELOW ZERO

Operating below zero
You have dropped from a status of a hero
And walking in a dark alley but narrow
Very soon you will wallow
In a mud of sorrow
Under the instruction of a pharaoh
If you want to sink deeper still
You are in for an ordeal
Where you have to kneel
In a dark dungeon studded with needles
Craving for a meal
You will be given mixed with silt

If however you want to come out of this rut
You need to climb a ladder with a dad
And shed out some of your characters shade
That makes you fly a jet
And assume an air of importance as you chat
At arrival, allow humility to have a place in your life net

SOLUTION FOR THE MOST SHAMEFUL VICES

Early morning
He was up with his fine netted crucible
Separating covetousness

Selfishness, envy and jealousy
From human body

From dawn to dusk
Nothing was successful
As they have been finely
Mixed with human nature
As sand is with sugar

Tired, he rested, pondered on the next move
And Ha! With a hurrah, he got a solution
He would give them some honorable names
So that they do not shame people
As they live with them

Love will stand in for covetousness
Self reliance will replace selfishness
And politics for envy and jealousy
With work accomplished, he went home
Had a nice meal and a sound sleep

LUCKY AND UNLUCKY

When conflict of interests clash
Two gentlemen; Lucky and Unlucky emerge
Distinguished by their walking gaits
And their countenance and demeanor
The fans of Lucky follow him rejoicing
While the fans of Unlucky do not

Lucky walks majestically
With a head high up
Distributing smiles here and there
Giving hands out inform of gifts
And praying and praising God for the fortune
He has not worked for

Unlucky walks with head bent
His eyes down cast
Defeated and despondent
His tail lodged between his hind legs
Cursing everyone including his gods
Because he has sown seeds he has not reaped

Nothing comes out of the blue
If you are lucky, you must be a compromise
For other people's misunderstanding
And if you are unlucky
You must be a victim of other
Peoples' plot and intrigues

UNIVERSAL DONOR V. UNIVERSAL RECIPIENT

Universal Donors give
And they do not expect to be given
They serve
And they do not expect to be served
They give sacrifices to others
And they do not expect others to give them sacrifices

Universal Recipients take
And they do not give
They are served
And they do not serve others
People die for them
And not ready to die for others

One is a servant, cool hearted and benevolent
The other is a master, hot tempered and selfish
You want to know them?
Trace the track record of their lives
And will not be difficult to know
And to welcome Mr. Universal Donor
To come and take care of your affairs
And to send away Mr. Universal Recipient
To go and take care of his own affairs

IF YOU WANT TO LIVE HAPPY

If you want to live happy
Never to be offended
By any life hiccup
How small it may be
Listen to this advice

When you want to be served
Consider every person your enemy
For that, you will appreciate
Any little goodwill service
Offered to you with a spoon

But if you consider everyone a friend
Owing them a right to serve you
You will be disappointed
Even when they serve you with a spade full

When you want to serve people
Consider every person your friend
For that you will serve everyone
Without discrimination
And get away with praises

But if you consider everyone an enemy
You will serve no one except your self
And everyone will turn away from you
Your payment will be condemnation and curses
As you live a life dotted with woes

THE EFFECT OF CORRUPTION

Find, search, spread your wings and fly
Drive, walk and find a friend to rely
Hungry, you better crawl and get a meat to fry
If you cannot ride a mule to try
And you will get before your spit dry
That corruption has two effects

One is to render some stupid
Because it has removed brains from them
They do not listen to logical advice
As they prefer to wallow in a mud like pigs
Instead of sleeping in a convenient bed and mattress

And they indulge in unprovoked laughter
Mimicking a schizophrenic in ecstasy

Another effect is to render some wise
Because it has seasoned them with spice
They abandon all ways
In favor of nursing new schemes
That places them above the others
As they are too wise
Their plans cannot be thwarted

SEEKING ADVICE

Time well invested is a time spent
 Seeking advice from a principled person
 As you will get a balanced advice
When realized will drive you
To a bastion of welfare
Your heart full of appreciation
When you catch his glimpse

Time wasted is the time spent
Seeking advice from an opportunist
As he will offer a bias advice
In favor of where his interest
Lies at that time
If you follow his advice
Will drag you to a dungeon of despair

Do not tell me you do not know
How to distinguish them from each other

The principled has statements tied to a mast
Even Tsunami cannot temper with it
In addition, he has steady eyeballs
Those do not swing from side to side
But focus on a subject he believes in so much

But an opportunist has shaky statements
That can be made to jump like ping pong
With a blow from the mouth
They can be swept away
In addition he has eye balls
Roving from side to side
Never get steady to capture a focus

FIRE SAFES

Nonsense
Do you think I'm stupid to put
My money again in your saving account
No, this time I shall put them in fire safes
Where ever there is fire accident
Even involving the whole concrete building
The money plus important documents shall still be safe

But what about investment
Don't you need it for your money?
How will your wealth grow?
Don't you want to get richer and richer?

I shall get rich by adding more
From the public funds

They will not know as I'm smart and tricky
Moreover I'm sure that
I shall not leave public position
Until I say goodbye to this life
By the way can we have a cup of coffee at Sheraton?

AVARICE

He stood akimbo
Watching the dowry inform of cows
Recently brought
For the marriage of his daughter
He counted 50
And cried to the top of his voice
Requesting more

When he was given another 30
He squatted
Bury his head between his legs
To attract attention and got 100
He then agreed to handover her daughter

But when another candidate
Approached and blamed him
For not waiting for him
As he was going to offer 200
He revoked the marriage
And gave his daughter away
For the new applicant

People wonder how long
He will continue making
And breaking marriages
If other better bidders
Were there applying

GUESS WHO I AM?

When I'm in difficulties
I need people to help me
Even my opponent
If God can make him forgive
I do promise to remember the names
Of those who have extended their hands
With a secret vow to return their services

But when difficulties are over
I would forget all the promises
Their names and their services
As I'm strong and wealthy
I would do what
My whims command
Guess who I'm?

This is a serious and dangerous test
Will it not spoil our relations?
If I say the truth
I'm afraid you are a devil incarnate
As it is only the devil that can deceive
People and go away with it
Am I right my true friend?

COOPERATION

Fire and water are staunch enemies
When they collide
As one touches the other
Hissing sound of wail
And gases fill the air
Yet they cooperate to cook a meal
Being separated only by a thin layer
Of a cooking utensil

As for people
They tend to get embroiled in relentless
Fighting and quarrellings
Even though they are separated
By wide borders and boundaries of land
Even those nations that say they unite
They are still involved in underground
Sabotage and intrigues

If non living enemies can cooperate
What about people?
Although they are provided
With intelligence by Mother Nature
Yet they fail to use it effectively for their welfare
And yet they claim to be masters
Of all living and non living things
Is it not a miscarriage of a duty bestowed by Nature?

DR. BELLARIO AHOY NGONG GENG

THE VALUE ONE GIVES TO HIMSELF

The value one gives to himself
Is more than what others give him
He wonders why he is not recognized
To handle certain task
While to himself, he thinks he can handle
Is it because he puts his interest above anyone else?

Yes, that is one aspect
And the other is the employer
He puts his interest above the others also
When two interests meet they employ each other
And when the two interests divert
They reject each other
Even if the other is more qualified for a job

Heaven forbids!
Selfishness is the culprit
And not the low qualification
Selfishness you go away
Go and divert to the leeway
And allow merit to sway

But that is the wishful thinking
I, the selfishness will never go away
Leaving my abode, the people behind
The time I shall disappear
Human beings will disappear too

COLD HATRED

I never knew him
Until I met him face to face
Executing an evil act against me
Stunned, I never believe he was the one
For I knew him a good man

As his innocence and humble look displays
And for the other reason for sure
He was staying with me
Living in the same compound
And sharing the same meal

What I knew of hatred
Was the one I now call hot hatred
To differentiate it
From the newly discovered
Cold hatred

It is hot because it unleashes its vile directly
And withdraws to its abode
A distance away
And to come back again more fiercely
Until either he wins or defeated

The good of this scenario is its direct approach
As it gives one a space and time to fight back
Beware of cold hatred
As it hides and does not give
Time to fight back

It sounds like you are talking about HIV
Because it is he among all carriers of hatreds
That lives with human beings
Enters its cells
And causes havoc call AIDS

Never, I'm talking about human hatred
The hot one fights one headlong
The cold one lives with one
He may use the throat as his abode
Never to be swallowed or to be vomited off

A COWARD

A coward is the one who makes
The safety margin so wide
Never give responsibility to a coward
For even when the danger is still far
He will run into panic

Nearer still
He will hide behind a child for cover
And climb on a bush twig
Thinking that he has climbed a tall tree
To escape danger

Or walk with the eyes downcast
Because he thinks the danger
Is looking for his eyes
Or vomit and drink its vomits
As he cannot go out to look for food
For fear of meeting danger

If you want to give him a responsibility at all
Give him a responsibility to eat
While standing at noon
Never in the morning
Or in the afternoon
Because he also fears his shadows

ENEMY POSING AS A FRIEND

An enemy posing as a friend
Does not appeal to objective interests
But subjective ones
Of a target to get his prey
He applies them cautiously
And intelligently
Without showing his emotions

A bit by bit
He gets nearer to the heart
Of the target
And waits for an opportunity
To pierce the target heart
Before he settles on the throne
The goal of his intrigues

Do not expose your subjective interests
Oh person of public affairs!
Lest you become a victim of an enemy
Posing as a friend
If you want to expose anything
Then expose your objective interests
For then you will get a friend posing as an enemy

DR. BELLARIO AHOY NGONG GENG

RELATION BETWEEN STYLE OF LIVING AND DEATH

When living a bad life
It is an invitation for your enemies to arrive
All connive to brandish their knives
You are nearer death by inches five

When living a comfortable life
All your enemies multiply by type
You have to keep wiping your face with sweat
You are nearer death by a distance to your wife

When living a moderate life
Your enemies are fewer than branches of olive
There is time for your crops to ripe
You are far from death by a long pipe

WORLD WITHOUT MARRIAGE

Think of a world without marriages
Promiscuous sexual relation will be in a barrage
Female rape and insecurity underlies miscarriages
And male rivalry over females in a deluge

To a female parent children will be born
Having only maternal identity like rhino horn
Blood related children can be in fond
As parental relationship is torn

That society will be weak
As it will have no confidence to kick

It will always remain sick
Unable to pick a tool and dig

MARRIAGE

Different sexes in union
This is a union in diversity in tune
In order to repro create a new generation
And to reduce problems numbering trillions

Without marriages life will be in disorder
Like a person falling from a ladder
The impact will be greater
And broken bones will be scattered further

If humankind has to reach life summit
It will have to strengthen marriages' permits
To be stronger and well knit
At that time only the sky will be the limit

POWER, RICHES AND PRIDE

I'm Power Crooker
My twin mate is Richer Crooker
Never step nearer
Unless you stoop lower
To shine my shoes cover

I walk with my head upright
Do not ask me for a ride

While your pocket is hopelessly dried
For that will injure my pride
Before Angela my bride

To lesser folks I'm blind
Their friendship I decline
For they have no match to my line
As they are maligned
They embarrass me before clients

TELLING TRUTH

Telling truth relieves burden
And makes one nearer to garden of Aden
It is the principle icon
To be touched by a deserved maiden

Telling truth can also make one shameful
When it reveals realities of one's short fall
The powerful can make you produce wails
When bitterness of truth proves harmful

Truth can make you being loved
Its essence can make mounts move
But can also make one being shoved
For revealing dark sides of doves

TELLING FALSE

Telling false condemns innocent
With no connection to a crime essence
And honors criminal giants
With blood smearing up their hands

Telling false erases credibility
That one enjoys in a community
And reduces self worth dignity
That is the flower of life in eternity

But false telling can saves lives sometimes
When you have to separate parties from clashing headlong
Like when you falsely inform one party in ambush line
That the other party is postponing for another time

PERSONALITY CLASH

Those with dignity can endure conditions
And ready to die to uphold their opinions
When they get fortune
Can assist others in ruin

Those with forsaken dignity
Suffer adverse conditions beyond pity
They become opportunists roaming a city
When they get fortune do not assist a needy

People with dignity deny themselves
But other people they help

People of no dignity are like wolves
They devour anything on the shelves

FELLOW HUMAN, A DOUBLE EDGED SWORD

Fellow human you are a double edged sword
At one edge your cuts produce joyous reward
At the other your cuts make a painful award
All due to complexity of your natural code

With you one thing is crystal clear
You give a joyful cut to bear
When your interest demands are there
No matter how averse they are to others far and near

You give a painful cut
When your interest demands are at stake flat
No matter how good they are to others' blood
To put it blunt you are a selfish lot

KNOW THIS FACT SO FIRMLY

People who come to you and kneel
When you are strong with charm and spell
Are not the same people, as well
Who stay with you bold
When you are weak or in jail

When you are strong
It is opportunists and flatterers clique

That hovers around so long
Pretending to like and sing your song
While they rob you of resources and belongings

And when you are weak
Only real friends sit around from a day break
They seek of how to help you tick
If you want to know this group and pick
You must either first get in trouble or become sick

THE ADVICE OF GRAND MA FISH (I)
(A dialogue between offspring and Grandma)

Offspring:
"Grand Ma we gather before you by Christ
 With tears rolling out of our eyes
To seek your advice so wise
We are melting away like ice
Being finished by an enemy in disguise

This enemy uses many tactics of cat
To get us like rat
And move us out of our water habitat
We do not know yet
What they do with our body parts

The situation is gloom and grim
As many fishes have stopped even to dream
Of reproducing offspring cream
Afraid of being carried away at whim
By the same enemy hunting in team"

Grand Ma:
"Oh offspring of my bosom
Whom I produce to blossom
To continue our existence with freedom
And achieve the purpose of our Creator Kingdom
When HE created and settled us here as home

What terrible thing you are saying?
Dying so early before growing?
And in great numbers in short timing?
I'm greatly worried my offspring
How did they get you? If you were not straying

Let me get my notebook and a pen
And leave my door open
For water to enter in torrent
Bringing along food particles I need often
To replenish my energy as much as I want"

THE ADVICE OF GRAND MA FISH (II)
(A dialogue between offspring and Grandma)

Offspring:
"One way is when in water they place
A hook connected with a lace
Lowered down loaded with terrine
And when we grab it with grace
We are hooked away without trace

Another they spread food and lay
On our hiding bay

And when serving ourselves with joy
They spread a net over without delay
And carry us wantonly away

Other, they array themselves near
In a wide circle the shape of a pear
Striking water with a fishing spears
Making our escape dire
Then they kill and drag us with tears
Grand Ma:
"Listen to me children of my blood
All the reasons you stated with bad mood
Are connected to where you get food
What is killing you is your appetite load
Pushing you to race for loot

The fact is that glare
Food does not sit in isolation in the air
It resides at the neighborhood of danger
Plainly where there is food there is danger on alert
That is a crucial lesson you must not ignore

Here is the valuable advice I can offer
If you take it you live longer
Ignore, you continue to die in numbers
As I do, eat food brought by current nature
And avoid food brought by alien givers"

DR. BELLARIO AHOY NGONG GENG

WHEN IT IS TOO DARK
(The Almighty will not leave you alone)

When conditions are too dark
Do not run into panic jerks
And do not predict black
The end of the World Ark
Or think that a day will never break

When it is at night, wake!
And look up the sky and check
There, you will see the stars well marked
And bright stark
Than any other day back

When it is a day, look for appreciation around
You will realize you are two in one
One is your dear self crowned
And the other is your shadow clone
The Almighty will never leave you alone

WHO ARE THE WORST ENEMIES

The best friend turns against you
Is your worst foe
Because he knows your hues
As well as your lows

Thus the saying teaches you to muster
"He who knows you better
Can serve you nicer
Or can bring you disaster"

Look for friends, they can be supportive
And they are good and effective
But be careful not to lose them collective
For they can be destructive

AN EXEMPLARY SCHOLAR

I'm exemplary scholar, smart and intact
For my studies I chose subjects
For profession of respect
I pray GOD to crown this with impact

As my studies are valuable
Because they apply to life gamble
In practice and benefit level
Time flies like the fastest plane double

At the end my efforts measure to my girth
Are to be compensated to my teeth
Inform of services and wealth
Before I embrace death

A THIEF LIKES AND DISLIKES

A thief engages in theft
But does not like to be ridiculed at
And to be called a thief brat
He likes to be famous noble and bright

A thief steals properties of others
But never like even brothers
To steal his properties to reward a mother
If he gets them, he would tear them to tatters

A thief deceives a victim
But he does not like at any time
To be deceived by others at whim
He likes to be treated fairly like them

SAY AND DO

Those who say one thing
And say the opposite without blinking
Are untrustworthy in the making
How can I say I'm going for a walk?
And again say I'm going to sleep

Those who say one thing
And do the opposite winking
Are hypocrites at work
How can I say I shall support her to win
And work for her to lose

Those who do one thing
And do the opposite blinking
Are insane without knowing
How can I indulge in laughing?
And at the same time crying

Those who say one thing
And do the same singing
Are wise and blooming
Like I say criminals deserve punishment
And not long they will be clinging
To bars with teeth gnashing

WHEN NIGHT IS LONGER THAN DAY

When night is longer than day
And feel every minute ticking away
While you turn in bed like a key
As sleep flies away beyond in sky

You are either spending a night
In one of the earth poles site
Or experiencing a pain bite
Under an influence of a disease smite

You may be exhaustively crunching
Either after a hard exertion or working
Or you are seriously grappling
With a difficult problem tackling

WHEN DAY IS LONGER THAN NIGHT

When day is longer than night
And feel as if time has died
With wind and air stopping right
While you sit there watching boys' kite

You are either spending a day
In one of the earth poles site
Or have ran out of a day program only
Or a program is not lovely
Or you do not have resources to do it jointly
Or your friends made you lonely

Approach the Eagle king
And to fly, you borrow wings
And in a loud voice you sing
To enjoy melody the national anthem brings

WHEN YOU FEEL BETRAYED

When you feel betrayed
Discouragement seizes you straight
Urging you to stop efforts arrayed
To implement a plan you create

Further betrayal mess
Will lead to a feeling of hopelessness
Coercing you to change a direction headless
Even if it is against your willingness

More betrayal will lead one to revenge
After making a U turn with rage
Former objectives are abandoned at a bench
In favor of cruising a new course to a trench

LOVE AND HATRED

Love walks in friendship with music fans
It attends music parties' bands
And music attends loves' indulgence
All happen in atmosphere laden
With delight and amusement

Hatred walks in friendship with selfishness
When hatred laughs selfishness laughs to foolishness
They attend each other parties with mindlessness
And share the same experiences harnessed
With sweet memories of being one time jobless

But when love meets with hatred close
The anger among them rises and glows
They nearly exchange blows
But remembering GOD's clause
They exchange pretended smiles short of hello's

GOOD AND BAD LUCK

Luck, good or bad
Rotates around a person hut
And revolves so glad
Around the larger community net
It runs in continuum dots
Never stop at any time to chat

However it seems to stick
More longer with some clique

Than other picks
The reason lies strict
With other events happening in league
When pros and cons bombard each other tricks

When good luck knocks your door step
Kiss it deep with your lips
For it will leave as time ticks
And when bad luck strikes at you deep
Recoils back and retrace your trip
For time will remove it with a whip

INDIVIDUAL AND PUBLIC INTEREST

Individual and public interests even if in a dialogue
Are components of one flock
Individual interest constitutes the blocks
On which public interest is built into rock

The logic is to satisfy first
The individual interest best
And public interest next
Will take care of its self

But it is not easy to satisfy with all respect
Every individual interest even from foot to neck
If you could satisfy group up to their back
You would do justice perfect

CHOOSING BETWEEN DIFFICULT AND EASY LIFE

On one side of a fence resides difficult life
Where one is born necked and deprived
Struggling with diseases of childhood type
Acquiring knowledge and skill enough
In order to get job for money drive

On the other side of a fence is easy life
Where one is a master of oneself
Alone thriving like a beehive
Living happy with a bride
And enjoy the company of his tribe

A barbed wire fence separates the two
To penetrate you must force yourself through
Fearing, your lamenting will grow
Courageous, you will pass a hole narrow
It is at a distance throw

WATCH OUT FOR GREAT EVENT!

When you see four meat eating animals
Lion, hyena, crocodiles and leopard as pals
Walking together in friendship cult
Then watch out Armageddon may be around a wall
Ushering in post Armageddon spell

Where in that era all of them are given a promise to survive
And that the Creator will either make division exclusive
By dividing all meat animals to each of them to live

Or will make them vegetarians each in its own drive
There will be no need for each other to cause strife

This can be a cause of sounding an alarm bell
For if the meat giants with a Creator have a deal
Then it is time to embrace hell
Or sink in a well
Leaving them to enjoy a smell

THINGS AND THEIR VALUES

Toil, sweat and struggle my friend
For worth and value you will gain
As value is buried deep down
In the earth and in the brains
For the worthy to find with strain

Yawn, sleep and stagger feeble
To lose worth and value simple
For everything valueless is available
Anywhere anytime double
Without engaging the brain cables

Think, ponder and comprehend
Anything that has value cent
Has tendency to be rare and in high demand
And anything that has lost value is stunted
Never to be demanded even on free grant

NATURE IN LIFE & POEMS

COMFORT AND DANGER ARE NEIGHBORS

Are you looking for comfort?
It is possible it may fill your court
But when you get it a lot
You attract danger on board
For you will be laden with envy of all sorts

Beware when comfortable
Make your fence thick double
And make the height above normal triple
To prevent neighbor posing noble
To unleash upheaval of evil

He will never leave you
So comfortable to row
Even when you present a cow
And a tray full of honey comb
Being carried by sister-in-law

THE GREATEST AND WORST OF THINGS

The greatest fear is fear from your shadow
The greatest folly is to terminate your life any how
The greatest waste of time is to worry about death
The worst love is to love your gallows

The greatest plot is to plot against your feathers
The greatest betrayal is to betray self servers
The greatest courage is to die for others
The greatest ungratefulness is to bite a figure of your tipper

DR. BELLARIO AHOY NGONG GENG

The serious sin is to pretend to pray with heart barren
The worst vice is to pretend to be different
The worst friendship is to let alcohol be your friend
The worst behavior is pride endorsed by parents

CONSEQUENCES OF FEAR

Fear! Fear! Fear!
Do not come near
For you throw great people to shame gear
And plunge their dignities into abyss sphere
Never recover for the rest of life years

Once a man approached a house his own
To find that waiting for him was a lion
Mouth wide, canines sharp, claws so positioned
And making a terrible noise heard in all directions
Putting a man in greater fear condition

To please the lion he attempted to blub
Throwing down his spears and clubs
But the lion was still so fierce as if clubbed
He then undressed and threw his clothes up
Yet the animal was still unmovable as if on trap

When he wanted to surrender his under wear
His wife intervened and rescued him at the rear
Hitting the lion with a glowing end of fire wood near its ears
And so dignity came back accompanied by stars
To resettle where he escaped because of fear

GATES OF RICHES

Riches has many gates like those of beaches
They are arranged in order separated by inches
From ground floor to the uppermost reaches
You can enter any gate as the goal is to get riches
All are decorated with golden stitches

While strategies of getting riches are different
The efforts put in are the same and apparent
Whether you are putting in a big capital like land
Or small capital such as a hen
To be managed by a faithful hand

Alas! When you are forced to come out like a rat
You must do so from one gate
Unlike the emergency gate of a jet
There is no parachute to act as a net
You must then fall with a resounding thud

THINGS AND THEIR OPPOSITES

Love is sweet when it is in close jar
Bitter when it splits a jar asunder with despair
Life is handsome when it is seen from far
Ugly when near and you have to kiss its rear

People like to be given appreciation
For a little service they have rendered
But loathe appreciating other good hearts
That has labored for them so hard

All people hate mistreatment obviously
But some of them have tendency
To mistreat others deliberately
Even on appeal of clemency

CRYING IN THE WILDERNESS FOR HELP

Oh come! My dear Oh come!
Come and help to solve prompt
The riddle I'm facing at home
 At large in the community bosom
Are those who dislike even my name
But difficult to know them

I wish to know before the sun goes down
So that I can protect myself
And be able to walk in the light of moon
In the path of my own
Clear and bright like noon
Oh come! My dear Oh come!

I need not come my dear
For I cannot be seen clear
But can be heard with ears
If you observe so far
This simple rule I'm saying
You will not miss knowing them

Observe those people in question
For a long time occasion
Meanwhile watch their actions towards you

Of deeds and omissions
You will never miss at conclusion
What you need under Mount Zion

WHO DOES NOT HAVE ENEMIES?

Everyone has enemies
Even the dead lying in peace
Their enemies just stop few degrees
Short of following them to grave abyss
Also the unborn in the womb nest
They have their enemies waiting with unease
To avenge mistakes committed by their race

Nonsense! Never put rubbish in a boat
What about those lots?
Who are true believers of God?
Those who defy odds
To obey the Ten Commandments taught
Conduct religious prayers in both bad and good
And help others out of woods

They too have enemies man!
From those who envy them in the land
For being living saints
And those who perceive with bad intent
Their interests stand
Being blocked by them and buried in a sand
Whether this is true or out of sense

DR. BELLARIO AHOY NGONG GENG

YESTERDAY A GIRL TODAY A WOMAN

Yesterday I was a girl
Today I'm a woman
What happened?
Can I be a girl again?

As for the boy
Yesterday a boy
Today a man
And can be a boy again
What is this injustice?
How can a river current
Run forth and back
As if in a pool under rapids
Is a boy a pool of rapids?

I must find out
If it is done by culture
I shall fight it tooth and nail
But if it is nature
I can do nothing
As no one with sense
Can fight its mother

TRUTH AND LIE UNDER DICTATORSHIP

Truth under dictatorship coils and recoils
Face down cast
He walks with a tail lodged between its hind legs
Not to see any face, not to shake any hands

And not to talk to anyone
Because of stigma of shame tagged to his face

As for a lie
He walks majestically
Between dark alleys of power
His head high up as the sky is the limit
With tail stuck out, waging and waving to anyone
That has crossed his way

Here is Mr. Lie turned truth
As it is known
The only way to make lie to become truth
 Is to repeat the lie many times
With a big club behind
To scare away those in doubt

WHY EDUCATION IS IMPORTANT

Educated person looks
Several years back
And several years ahead
Before taking decisions
In most cases errors are few

Uneducated person looks
For the years of his life
Which are some few years back
And few years ahead
Most decisions are in error

Like a person standing on high ground
Educated person sees wider horizon
Than the one on lower ground
Before he decides
In most cases the angle of error is narrow
Likewise on viewing things
The less educated looks at the back of his feet
As a result the angle of error in making decisions is wider
These are the people who make decisions and change them
In fact they vomit and swallow again their vomits

TOO MUCH FEAR

Too much fear
Without appropriate gear
Can produce many tears
Many more when it is influenced by beer
Because the cause of fear hides at the rear
Not exposing itself so clear

When the situation like that appears
Better study the cause from all corners
Without neglecting looking into the jar
As it can hide its body except the ears
Once known, fear
Will run away for his life so dear
Giving you a space to breathe and hear

Have you not learned Oh Dear!
That knowledge is power?
Many people unaware do not care

If knowledge can send objects to Mars
Don't you think it can cause fear to veer?
It can do so with sheers
Sending fear so far to join its peers

NEPOTISM

Mr. Corruption
Who is Nepotism?
Why is he ever healthy, ever happy?
While others groan in pain

Nepotism gets unfair advantage
Over his colleagues especially in employment
From his powerful relative
To put it blunt, from me

But what about those who do not get
Unfair advantages from their relatives?
And instead they deny them jobs
How do you call them?

You mean the self-denial group?
These are people self inflicting themselves
In order to earn good names from others
We give them the name of nincompoop

DR. BELLARIO AHOY NGONG GENG

WHETHER TO HAVE A GRAVE OR A PLACE

Every living person will have a grave
It may be in a stomach
Of a carnivore, fish, bird of prey
Or under the ground
Properly laid
And covered with stones
Some with roses

But not every dead person
Will have a place on earth
This is reserved for those who were able
To tingle the nerves of the earth
Squeeze the tasty juice out of it
And if God's will, they would like to return back
To them Earth was heaven

As for the rest they have to cling
To Almighty feet praying
Not to allow them
To return to earth
To relive the nasty experiences
They had
To them, earth was hell

THE MOTHER OF INTEGRITY IS DEAD

Always from this mansion comes out a lad well dressed
Well combed and walking majestically to a waiting car
His physical features are not attractive

Yet he commands the respect of his age mates
They bow down in reverence
On seeing him
Did I hear that they call him Corruption?

Also from a small compound, comes out a lad
I heard people calling him Integrity
Handsome and composed
But wears rags with no shoes
He does not usually take bath
Eyes and nose full of body secretions
Those attract no body except flies

You man of weird thinking
Why don't you usually
Understand the differences?
Even from the obvious
Corruption is well taken care of by its mother
While the mother of Integrity is dead

INTELLECTUAL

You might have had education any way
But important is to be a deep and a critical thinker
Weighing issues from bottom to the top
And from side to side
Burrowing deep to the hollow of issues
Before coming back to the common pool of senses
Yet no one will notice because your intellect has buried you

You might have roamed the whole world
Fell short of ascending to moon
And knowledgeable enough
Not to approach the sun
To avoid turning to gases
At the first sensation
Yet no one will notice you because your intellect has buried you

Intellect
The ability to know things
Has made your color bright white
You thought that would make you visible
For a reasonable eye to see
And for a shrewd mind to appreciate
Yet no one will notice you because your intellect has buried you

Do you want to be visible? Come on
Damn your intellectual brightness
Turn your head downwards
And the legs to point upwards
Use the legs to think and use the hands to walk
There you will be noticed and clearly seen
How happy you will be!

PRICE FOR DECEPTION

Price for deception is loss of credibility
No one believes what he says
But how can one be without credibility

When this is a quality of gallantry
Left to thieves, uncouth and riff raffs

Price for deception is the cutting of a tongue
So that there will be no one
To convey the message
But how can one survive without tongue?
Unless one is among some birds of prey, the crows

Price for deception is loss of popularity
This is bad news to those who endear
Dignity, integrity and self esteem
As for lovers of avarice
They have thick skins to sense that loss

GOOD BYE SUN

From where water lilies bath
And laugh with winds blowing
From a north westerly direction
The lilies had just bent to kiss water in love
And when they stood erect
They found the sun has just passed them
Moving towards the westerly direction

The lilies want to follow
But had no feet to walk or run
And so they sent the clouds after
In vain attempt to catch him
But he was gone
Without delay he armed himself with rays
And asked the stars to follow

They marched, flew and landed
At the end they reached the destination
It was the heaven gate
There was a serious consultation with the owner
At last the sun was the only one allowed to enter
Leaving the stars to raise a bitter hand wave
Good bye Sun!

TYPES OF INJUSTICES

Take a wage, hard won by a worker
And squander it without eye blink
There, you are engaged in injustice
But injustices are so many
And of so many kinds and types
Like stars you can't count
But among those, the worst type
Is the one caused by your own kind

Injustices are like lethal arrows
If you send them to your foes
You don't feel
To sympathize with a victim
And if sent against you
You wince under their multiple pains
But among those, the worst type
Is the one sent by your own kind

Many try to fight injustices
With tooth and nail
Some succeed as they pass it on
Others fail miserably

They squeak, yell, rant and rave
With no one coming to their rescue
But among those, the worst type
Is the one caused by your own kind

BELOW THE CAUSES FOR MISUNDERSTANDING

They clash, rant and roar
Before parting ways
The ombudsmen intervened
But with no avail
It needs wisdom of a scientist
To search and research

For below the causes for misunderstanding
Are deep and real causes

The causes are secret, they can't be told
Without losing credibility and dignity
For they touch the bones and the umbilical cords
But they will only talk of superficialities
Which even a fool can dismiss as childish
The causes have not been unearthed

For below the causes for misunderstanding
Are deep and real causes

Never waste time reconciling those quarreling
Especially when they present trivialities
While as you know them
Are adult, educated, civilized and well to do

Measures they take are inappropriate
Waiting for a chance to be on each other throat

For below the causes for misunderstanding
Are deep and real causes

DOING WRONG

Doing wrong is awful
Condemned by all sensible people
As it violates rights of others
Making life unbearably uncomfortable
The act is committed mindlessly
Without regret or remorse

Rarely does a person believe he is doing wrong

When committing wrong
The perpetrator with no shame
Places his head between his legs
And looks only at the hollow
Between his buttocks
He does not care for the rights of others

Rarely does a person believe he is doing wrong

If only he could remember one dictum
To do to others
What he likes them
To do for him
This world would be safe and secured

But he does otherwise

Rarely does a person believe he is doing wrong

TARGET OF CONSPIRACY

My wings are clipped
Legs strained with a rope
And mouth stitched
I cannot fly, walk or eat
Just because I have skills
To tame life
For that reason I'm a target of conspiracy

My properties got destroyed
My loved one hood winked to rebel
Children lured to drug addiction
All these were products of my labor
Blood and sweat I invested
This stirred in them envy and jealousy
For that reason I'm a target of conspiracy

I wonder what next I could do
To appease them
I decided to arranged a table with food and drinks
When I invited them into a hall, they were not there
And when I looked back on the table it was flat empty
Who are they? Are they demons from Lucifer?
May be for that reason I'm a target for conspiracy

DR. BELLARIO AHOY NGONG GENG

VICTIMS OF INDIRECT CAUSES

Pity and sympathy goes to people
Those die due to a far and untraceable cause
As there are no laws meted out for them
They die as a result of negligence or mismanagement

Have you ever sued a bird in court for burning a house?
Or politicians for not budgeting for a mother
To avoid losing a child at birth
Or a Doctor for not attending to a bleeding patient until he dies
Or a leader causing people to die to keep himself in power

Of all human causes of death they are the majority
What little is covered by law!
And how large and extensive is left to chance!
Can Almighty come to their rescue?

WHAT HURTS MOST

What hurts most is the injustice
From those you struggle with
To achieve a common goal
What hurts most is the disrespect
Shown by those you love
So much that there is no other alternative

What hurts most is the disregard
From the fellow comrades
Whom you have highly regarded and helped
What hurts most is when your friends

You have served at the time of their need
Disown you at the time of your need

What hurts most is when you do not get appreciation
From those you have sacrificed so much
With scars of your involvement so visible
What hurts most is when a person talks ill of a dead person
He never considers that one time he will also die
Leaving some social debt behind

What hurts most is when children
Innocent as they are
Are uncared for
What hurts most is when the elderly
With all their services and sacrifices
Are mistreated by the young

CONFRONTING AN OPPONENT

When confronting an opponent
Do not do to his advantage

When he cries
Do not cry
For if you do
People will consider both of you
To be in pain
They will advise all of you
To see a Doctor

When he laughs
Do not laugh
For if you do
People will consider both of you happy
They will leave you both to enjoy your time

When he kicks you
Do not kick him
For when you do
People will take both of you
To be culprits
They will place both of you in a police cell
Until the next day

Better do opposites of his actions
When he cries you laugh
When he laughs you cry
And when he kicks you complain
With that people will notice the difference
And will place judgment appropriately

TO THE ISLAND OF NO RETURN

Celebrate with joy and happiness
Knocking all doors and search
Everywhere to catch the glimpse
Of the person who set you free
So that you can kneel down
And thank him
But this man you love is not here
He has gone to the island of no return

You want to meet him and complain
About plethora of problems
Those have bedeviled you
Since the birth of freedom
They are in a nutshell
Prioritize as Security, Education, Food and Health
However this man you love is not here
He has gone to the island of no return

You complain to ears that cannot hear
As they are blocked by wax of parochialism
And appeal to eyes that cannot see
Since they are blindfolded by selfishness
Why look stunned and surprised?
Those good ears and eyes you knew have gone away
With a person who cares
That one has gone to the island of no return

ALCOHOL EFFECT

I'm alcohol, I hold friends tightened
Since time dawned at Aden
I was created hidden
Not direct like other foods eaten

I do not look for people
But people look for my eye ball
For when I'm with them on a table
Dignity leaves the room humbled

On my company way
People easily develop friendship bay
They can also develop quarrels bray
Which they forget the other day

INJUSTICE IS UNCONQUERABLE

Among races and nations injustice prevails
Attempts are made to put it in jail
En route to devouring hell
But in vain it escapes waging its long tail
Causing anguish and wails

Among tribes and clans it causes havoc
Hatred and jealousies it provokes
Even dogs are urged to mock
At the victims while they walk

Among families it can make discord
Attempts are made in court
But all the same it is difficult to sort
Only when you cannot utter a word
Can it be thrown over board

THE ROLE OF MONEY

When relations are too dark like a night
Rift so severe they trade cyanide
With both parties opting to use knives
Money can creep in to unite

Once they have to steal at night
And are supposed to share it right
But with loot some decided to hide
Money can awfully divide

When peace dwells
On people's will
And resources are there to fuel
Money is there to build

CHAPTER III

NATURE AND ITS FEATURES

THE CAUSE THAT HAS NO CAUSE

Every creation has a cause
That can be called a source
To produce effect in rows
This process can produce laws
Which nature uses on toasts

But there is a cause without cause
All knowledge stops at its nose
And return to the world of cause
And effect with bows
That cause is GOD boss

Its backyard cannot be known
Behind there is no town
And no one can search around
Or hear a sound
In it infinity abounds

A BRIDGE OF KNOWLEDGE

Against your zeal
It tempts your will
When financially downhill
It pays your bill
And drags you to hell

On God's seal
It plots a deal
Which if you yield
It can kill
That is the devil!

Its actions produce a wedge
So wide you can't see the edge
There is need of a bridge
To cross over for search and research
It is no other than the informed knowledge

GOOD AND BAD

Good on God's way travels
On the way smooth and devoid of gravels

It has to take care on arrival
For Almighty is vexed by grumble

Bad on devils way travels
On the way rough and laid with gravels
It has to wail and complain on arrival
Because the master entertains grumbles

How divergent are the two
If one has to open its jaw
The other one will stand in awe
And if one is to squat and do
The other visits a loo

RELIGION

On this planet humans are insecure
Unabated are wars
Spreading everywhere with terror
Which everyone deplores

Need then arose to look for the Creator
That brought them so far
So they can avoid danger with detour
Religion is the way back to the door

But alas! There are many like pieces of a comb
Some accept one and blow others with foam
Each accusing each other of leading to a doom
Not knowing that all roads lead to Rome

MILK

Milk is life supporting matter
Second only to water
The new born first food rater
And the first taken in life earlier
Rendering the health of a mammal better

Without liquid milk
Life of a quarter creations cannot tick
The life crucible will leak
Rendering the nature weak
And permanently ill

Milk is a gift from the Creator
It is an oar
That crosses the life boat over the river shore
The characteristics it bore
Renders it useful even when sour

SLEEP AND DEATH

Sleep is a conscious mind at rest
After working the whole day from dawn to dusk
All voluntary organs are tied to a mast
Leaving the involuntary alive until body is sent to dust

Death is both conscious and unconscious mind
At rest with the fallen giant
Body and soul cannot be recovered to dine
Except when religion makes it to rise again

At that time science will stand at God's gate shivering
For not properly comprehending the Almighty's teachings
Science wants to return for more learning
But the Almighty told him to learn more from hell wailing

JOURNEY FROM INFINITY AND BACK

I came from infinity
Where lodges trinity
In perfect unity
And exuberant air of dignity

Once as I was playing in water, I dived
To find myself alive
Now I'm resting with my wife
In what is called life

I'm going back to infinity
With all the life niceties
What I have found is vanity
Bordering insanity

But the Almighty told me succinctly
To continue staying with life purposely
Until he calls me back discretionally
He could not tell me the time exactly

Obeying orders for staying
I decided to engage in life chasing
I almost caught it but it slipped away missing
Leaving me in the world guessing

Unable to get life due to bad luck
I appealed to Almighty to have me back
I needed to get my belongings packed
But life refused saying
"I was not worthy of any except my neck"!

LIFE IS A DREAM

Once at my prime
And after having eaten to a brim
I retired on a wooden bed frame
And had the following dream

I found myself in my mother womb
Enclosed in a case shape of a dome
And floating on a lake serene and warm
At a sudden a lake discharged me to a large home

I met many obstacles
My first experience was to suckle
In order to surmount hurdles
That lied ahead to be tackled

One time I felt mature enough to marry
The in-laws gave me a handful of worry
Because they demanded a lot of dowry
This could not be put together in a hurry

At last the deal was sealed
As the future was built
The womb of the new bride yielded
And the product was real

As children grew older
They became bolder
Some became soldiers
And others leaders

At that time I became an elder
The hair turned whiter
With a back curved and tougher
My body became weaker

And a walk became wider and frailer
The eyes began to see nearer
As I cannot read my folder
Even with a spectacle reader

When I wanted to straighten my back erect
I heard a crack
And there was a fatal break
That woke me up to ride a waiting truck

WHAT ARE WE?

On taste scale we are bitter
We repulse anyone strange to us faster
And want to be our own ever
But we are modified by sweet cover of culture

Compare to animals we are beasts
Surviving by preying on others for feasts
In the process we destroy their lives with ease
But we hide by wearing a human coat as nests

We are essentially devilish
We enjoy seeing one in anguish
And ready to plunge him into abyss
If we are not being restrained by a religious dish

WHERE IS MY TIME DAD?

Oh Creator! Half of my life time grant
Is taken by my parents plans
Grooming me to be like them blunt
And looking down at my frivolities trend

The other half is taken over
By my very children
Giving me worry fever
For what will be their future

Soon after I have accomplished that
I hear your knock at my door flat
Asking me to see you urgently right
Then where is my time Dad?

ROADS OF LIFE

One is born to the junction of two roads crossing
One road is short and straight at the beginning
Crooked at the end and winds up into a fathomless pit
Another road is long and zigzag at the beginning
But straight at the end led by the glorious wit

The former road is founded by lawlessness breed
Lined by bottles of alcohol and opium trees
And sprinkled with flowers of lust and greed
Where disorder and thuggery agreed
And to where pain and wails are freed

The latter one is founded on a creed of business
Lined by trees of trustworthiness
And sprinkled with perfume of equality and fairness
Order and peace control the process
Even bad events wear ceremonial dress

BEGINNING AND END

Beginning announces its arrival
Sirens are sounded formal
Flags are raised as usual
And hymns are sang by Generals

But End comes abruptly
One does not dress normally
Love ones are disowned unceremoniously
And precious articles are not stored correctly

What Wisdom!
Since end is always painful gloom
Announcing it would cause a commotion to roam
Causing love ones to bear the brand of doom

DR. BELLARIO AHOY NGONG GENG

TASTES OF LIFE

If you taste life so sweet at high degrees
That happens at someone expenses
Who may taste its bitter peas
At the same time of your bliss
Tears rolling from his eyes at ease

If you taste life bitter all the time being
Then someone somewhere is sucking
All the sweet part without blinking
Your rights are at the stream draining
You better struggle to the extent of pain taking

If you taste life sweet at a time
And bitter at other time
Then thank GOD
You are leading a balanced life in a boat
Where no one is crying foul of your load

LOOP OF LIFE

At the beginning you come alone in a boat
Necked and soaked in water and blood clot
Your midwife coddles you a lot
She cleanses and lays you in a cot

As you begin to sense you are in company
As they nick name you honey
Becoming mature you are with community
Next with your mate and children making life so funny

As you age company lessens
And begins to decline with fans
Until you are left alone in whine
To enter your grave in silence

FOOD

Stuff all living things long for so far
As you produce energy at the core
That life activity depends on more
Lack of you makes death roars

In abundance you are rude
Since you clog the system on load
Causing the condition of obesity to hood
Beckoning death to loot

You are beautiful in moderation suit
Neither lack of you nor abundance of you is good
But who cares to balance your equation boat
Unless one is in GOD incarnate mode

OUR COMMON NATURE VERSES OUR ARTIFICIAL CONCOCTION

All people irrespective of their parental rating
Are born necked and crying
Weak, poor and gasping
Without any belongings

During life some acquire statuses glitter
Over many others
They do so either through inheritance proper
Or through hard work or intrigues ever

When old they lose belongings and brain
As power wanes
At last they die dispossessed of belongings
Whether they were Kings or in chains

LIFE AMONG STARS

One beautiful and calm night
I was wandering observing the stars bright
Unaware I was lifted up by a device tight
To a distance among the stars heights
Rotating on an orbit of my own pride

What I found was intriguing
Stars of various sizes and shapes conversing
While orbiting the solar system in colorful parading
Each one beckoning me for a love partying
Which might had ended up in a wedding

When I wanted to join their party
Mother earth arrived in a hurry
And pressed me to its bosom tightly
Smacking me for straying carelessly
Lest I disappear into oblivion unwary

FORCES OF LIFE

Since birth, forces that act on a person life
Are of two groups in line
One group pushes a person to rise
And live longer to size
The other pulls a person down to demise

When forces of life are stronger
A person lives longer
But if forces of demise are tougher
A person is doomed to demise sooner
As quick as those forces can pull faster

Whether life forces are strong or not
The ultimate game is won right or wrong
By doom forces along
Since they are destined headlong
To send a person to the earth he belongs

SEEDS

Welcoming you with joy I spread out my hands
Oh! Secret of life on land
You go down to soil as one in ten
But come out in tenths and thousands

Without you there is no production tag
No economy and no life pack
Only an idiot cannot know your precious role
Since he has hidden his head between the legs

A farmer without seeds
Hurries to a grave with speed
While a farmer who have sown and weed
Crowns his life with golden beads

CHILDHOOD

Happy those days when I was a child
When everything I needed when I yelled,
Was provided free by my loved ones
From whom I hailed
After being adult
I must alone settle my bill

Happy those days when I was a child
When parents would kneel
Down tapping my heels
In order to produce a sleep yield
By that they took a role of a sleeping pill

Happy those days when I was a child
When mother coddled me mild
And inquired about my favorite meal
And protect me from being hurt by a hill
When will those days return to my life?

CHILDHOOD AND ADULTHOOD AT A BALANCE

When one is a child under care
He longs to be in a group of adult peers

In order to enjoy adult desires
Work to earn money and a car
To control his life wires

When one is an adult like Tom
And meeting conditions bothersome
He wished to become a child at home
Where he will enjoy usual love storm
Warmth of someones bosom

Here we are kissing wisdom at its nose
If child life was all advantageous
There would be no need wishing to grow up
And if adult life was all good without gathering moss
People would have skipped natural laws

COMPONENTS OF CONSCIOUSNESS AT A BALANCE

I'm sub conscious mind, I tell you
I'm made with you and born with you
But because I'm inadequate in skill
I gave up control to conscious mind jell
To cope with exigencies of this world

I'm conscious mind, I yell for everyone to hear
Without me you cannot cope with life in this world
I developed to render you reasonable, dignified and logical
Because this is a hard labor job, I kneel
And rest everyday leaving subconscious to work until you leave this world

I'm super conscious mind source
I'm not made like subconscious
Or developed like conscious
I'm there before and after creation of laws
Guess who I am? Before your nose

LIFE AFTER SEVENTY

Lives after seventy
And lives under five years are nieces
In both they are dependent like geese
On others to assist them with services
Vital to their lives stretches

Unlike under five
That could not prepare for future life
Seventies agers are supposed to have developed their beehives
But alas! Many people in our culture do not consider that in their lives
Pinning their hope on their children to make them thrive

What a folly John!
They will regret deep to their bones
If they commit that mistake on their own
It will not be long before they are gone
Cutting down their lives with moans and groans

ALL STAGES OF LIFE ARE WITH PROS AND CONS

When one is a child
He enjoys the delicacy of parents' meals
But is not free to do anything he wants
As he is under a control of someone's will

When he is an adult
He will taste a freedom salt
But will always get into life driven insults
He can face them not, because he is unskilled

When he is elderly
He will enjoy imparting knowledge wisely
But is weak to produce physically
Because his muscles are too weak to work properly

IN A DRILL WITH WILD ANIMALS (JOHN's EXPERIENCE)(I)

In a training session on animals conservation
That was being conducted by a nearby nation
Practically in a park of game population
An angry rhino attacked the trainees at the central location
And dispersed them in different directions

One John ran for his life defying gravity
But the animal left others and ran after him incessantly
At a high way road John ran under the bridge for safety
While the rhino stood outside with its horn towards John menacingly
It could not enter below a bridge because of its huge body

While John sat there speculating on what move the Rhino would make
He was surprised for below him was a strange movement like quake
Of something rolling out its body from his weight to save its neck
And to his surprise it stuck its neck out and Ha! It was a cobra snake
Ballooned with poison and anger, looking straight into John's eyes with rage

IN A DRILL WITH WILD ANIMALS (JOHN'S EXPERIENCE) (II)

John was now between two lethal foes
A rhino waiting to render him a dead mouse
If he tried to retrace its toes
And a snake sending him to death jaws
Following any slight movement of his shoes

With a split second makes
John decided to catch the serpent neck
With all his two hands connect
The snake then curled and wagged
And twisted its body around John's legs
Giving him electric vibrations with aches

With approach of game warders the rhino ran away in fright
But John unconscious was found with the snake dead in his hands
The warders could not remove the snake as the hands were too tight

Both of them were taken to a hospital at night
Where they were disentangled under anesthetic might

HIV/AIDS

It is HIV/AIDS
It has been a scourge of late
Since it appeared up to date
The body of its victim it ate
Until it is in the grave laid

Nations wonder what the remedy is
That cannot be found at ease
As the virus is clever and active like bees
It keeps changing its character like seas
Until it rests its victim in peace

However prevention tricks
Taken together can click
As ABC can kick
Followed by avoidance of pricks
And MTCT break

TREADING A MIDDLE PATH

Life is difficult, I must admit
If I go far left
I may fall in a pit
And if I move far right
I may tread on a shit

If I go far north
I may go back and forth
And if I go far south
I may together miss the earth
Two extremes cannot make life worth

Life worth seems to lodge in the middle
It may be too small to pass through a needle
Forcing it is an ordeal
But if I push a little
I may tap a liter

YOUTH

If life cycle were a river
Youth would have been its water
Carrying along fish and others that matter
Making life comfortable and softer

And if life cycle were a garden
Youth would have been likened
To the plants that grow unblemished
To flower and produce in abundance

But youth these days are bewildered a lot
By thrills of modern age fraud
Those have placed themselves at their throat
They neither swallow nor vomit them without blood

LIFE WITHOUT DEMAND AND SUPPLY

Imagine a world where every that tallies
Is self sufficient for life delicacies?
Never to demand or request supplies
From any other person or allies

Relations will cease to exist at most
As there will be no value to host
And life will have no immediate purpose
As it will not be worth living at any cost

Such a life will be utopian
As it is so strange to earth creation
It may exist elsewhere nearer the creator giant
Where aliens are its inhabitants

PROSECUTION OF MR. SCIENCE (S)
BY MR. RELIGION (R)

The voice of Mr. R bellowed in action
In a rally discussing the dogma of resurrection
The essence was to lay fears of the faithful congregation
Not to worry pitying their bodies when they die in submission

For the Almighty will raise them wholly by type
From the grave to witness judgment alive
The lucky ones to enjoy the blissful Heaven life
In response the faithful were nodding in unison drive

DR. BELLARIO AHOY NGONG GENG

Out of the blue Mr. S stepped in with a bang
Brandishing his sharp tongue
He reversed the whole scenario blank
By stating that bodies are reduced along

To their small elements when dead like a rock
To be used by nature as building blocks
To create other creatures flock
As time ticks, talks and walks

Mr. R was upset and furious
The speech was sacrilegious and dangerous
The next day Mr S body was found dangling posthumous
Below a rope tied to a tree branch. How curious?

REUNION WITH ANCESTORS

After ending my life mission
I went back to join my ancestors' haven
The journey was three days for a man
And four days for a woman
Exactly the days for burial ritual conclusion

I saw my ancestors queuing along the shores
In a ascending order welcoming me with choirs
My parents were the first to step out on the fore
As they were the ones to lead the introduction tours
They all introduced themselves until the first ancestors

To my surprise, the ape monkey parents came
Walking on four to welcome me at the cave

I was stunned and recalled deep
The Darwinian theory of evolution tape
Were Adam and Eve apes?

TWO LEGS OF LIFE

Life is sweet when it walks around
On two legs of hope and love fun
Its head faces up to up keep a golden crown
That can glitter when showered by sunshine
The top so high to be touched by any hand

Life is bitter when it turns upside down
And walks on its head touching the ground
To manifest hate no one has ever known
Its legs straining in tendency bound
To fly off to heaven before dawn

When that happens Life is worthless
Its owner struggles to pack up mindless
His belongings to return to the womb nest
That is not there, because to drive truth to press
The mother had died many years ago

LIFE AND HER TWO CHILDREN

Life has two children in her nest
One is called happiness
Born first
Another is called sadness

Born last
Both are strong and robust

Life decided to stay with happiness fondly
Leaving sadness lonely
This angered sadness greatly
So he devised a plan to kill happiness finally
By digging him a hole so deadly

Covered with a straw spread so sparsely

Happiness fell in at night and got killed
Life with no alternative deal
Went to live on sadness hill
With no shelter to shield
And so Life started with happiness thrill
And ended with sadness bill

REQUEST FOR A JOURNEY TO ETERNITY AND BACK

She prayed ardently
Asking favor from the Almighty
To grant her permission to visit eternity
When she had put much effort pleadingly
A deep voice bellowed from above encouragingly
 Allowing her to go only
After she has accepted below conditions voluntarily

"It is possible to visit eternity and back bound
Provided that you will first be broken down
Into invisible indivisible particles

Then after the visit round
You will come back after the particles clones
Have been reconstituted and sewn
Not as original self but in mutated form

Just as words are broken into letters discs
The same letters can form another word mutatis mutandis
Thus if you are going there in a character of a DOG
You may come back as OGD, ODG, DGO, GDO or GOD goodies
Never will you come back in your original DOG form as you insist
Do you still want to undertake your journey Miss?"
Her answer was big NO! She was just on light moment tease

REPENTANCE COMPLAINING TO ALMIGHTY

Oh Almighty!
When you gave me the mission to the world
I was to be taken by people to their hearts
So that they do not repeat
The same mistakes they had committed
By this, sin will dwindle and World will be free

Instead they keep me at their lips
And continue to repeat the same mistakes
Then I'm called again
Never allowed to enter the hearts
But to spend my time at the lips
Kicking my heels

DR. BELLARIO AHOY NGONG GENG

I'm tired, bored and hungry
For since I came to the earth
I had never ate, rested or slept quietly
Honestly I'm failing my mission utterly
And by that I fail your omnipotence greatly
By infallible right you should not fail honestly

My humble request is that
Either you take me back to your abode
To rest before taking me to another planet
Or you exchange the positions of hearts and lips
So that I can easily access
The hearts to accomplish my mission

I BELIEVE IN GOD MY CREATOR

I believe in God my Creator in heaven bay
The omnipotent, giver of power in a golden tray
The omniscience, giver of knowledge through a ray
Before I go to work everyday
And before I retire on bed, I pray

Because he is merciful sustained by wit
He always forgives me when on need
Especially for all blunders I commit
Including stealing wheat
Depriving others to eat

Look! For every time I have a sentence
After committing another crime by chance
He would stretch his arms to embrace

As it is divined to look for one lost sheep in the universe
Than take care of 99 sheep already in the fence

For this reason
God and I has covenant knitted nicely
I believe in God my Creator fondly
Why don't you try my life style seriously?
It is both humane and godly

WHETHER MOTHER NATURE IS GOOD OR BAD

Mother Nature will be good with you
When you respect her laws
And live in accordance
It will be angry if you do not obey them

But why does she punish without warning?
So that one is aware and avoids trouble
Its laws were established since creation
On the bases of if you respect you succeed
And if you disobey you fall
She has no time to give warnings every time

But you know what?
She is ever wise and stern at the same time
All knowledge of her laws
Are hidden
If you want to uncover them
Then search and research, learn and relearn

By that you will be in good books with the Mother Nature
The prize, you live the age assigned by HER

EXPLOITS OF NATURE

When danger is near
The frogs stop to croak
While the warning birds fearless
Hover making disturbing noises
Even at the expense of their lives

Dogs howl when danger is far
Bark when seen
And make a deep groan
When it is very near

Do politics exhibit the same phenomenon?
Yes they do
But politics being practiced by creatures
More complex in behavior than others
Out do it in a smarter way
As in essence the human creature
Took lessons from the animal world
They do not have capacity to perform beyond nature

BIRTH AND DEATH

Birth and death are two sides of one coin
On birth side are the groans from Pain
Mingled with hope and encouragement

Then the lull, the sigh of relief
The ululation and the naming

On the death side is the pain
The uncertainty, the loss of hope
The pause followed by wails
And the lowering down to the grave

The difference between them is that
The date of birth will be known by a person
When he has grown up later in life
But the date of death can never be known by a person
Even though a communicator follows him to the grave

BEHAVIOR OF LIFE

Life comes from somewhere
And lives in an abode
When hungry
He eats outside his abode
When he has nothing outside
He eats his abode
When abode is consumed up
He disappears into oblivion
From where he actually came

JOURNEY TO PEACE

My Creator instructed me
To go from his factory

To realm of peace
Before he calls me back
For another mission

I started from the womb to home
But found that it has been
Occupied by injustice
He then ordered me to fight injustice
In order to gain freedom

When I entered the Freedom realm, it was not there
But turned to hell by Lucifer
He instructed me more to fight Lucifer
 But how can I fight Lucifer
Without your intervention Oh Creator!

HEAVEN AND HELL ARE WITHIN US

Why do we scan every direction?
Looking for where heaven and hell are
Ponder, search and discern
In the process there are
Two components within us

One component is humane
It is considerate and full of compassion
This is by all means heaven
The other is devilish, anti-human and selfish
This is by all means hell

You mean heaven and hell are neighbors?
Yes, they are joined by a thin band
Seeing each other
But they will never unite
Even under one entity

DAYS ARE GONE AND OLD AGE IS BORN

Days are gone
And old age is born
What did you do on your own?
Before accompanying sun
Pass the noon
To the Western horizon

Surely no need to shed tears
On the time already buried
That will serve a lesson
To those still rising with a sun
To exert efforts and score goals

As for you, pose
Take in a deep breath
On your marks, get set and go
While collecting pearls after pearls
And gold after gold
Making use of skills and experience
Before going down with a sun set
After all, they say
It is better late than never

ORDER AND DISORDER
(Statements by Mr. Order and Mr. Disorder at the press conference)

Mr. Order:
"I'm Order with wisdom indivisible
With me commanding behind the table
Existence is organized from invisible to visible
And from small to big labels
Each having its own definition unquestionable
And moves along its own orbit and axis cycle
Even the bodies of living things at their levels
Are organized physically and functionally in a pattern incredible
And in such a way that mimics the pattern of marble

Without me there will be no existence in the universe
As everything will move haphazardly aimless
Bombarding each other in a terrible mess
Resulting in a turmoil and nothingness
I tell existence as bless
Would never have made the first step more the less
From the beginning over the hill crest
And people would not have existed at best
To listen to this statement I'm making in earnest"

Mr. Disorder:
"I'm Disorder
It is true the whole creation exists with Mr. Order
But some part of creation dubbed human beings prefer
To exist both with Mr. Order and me at the back door
Their first ancestor having committed at the creation border
So called cardinal sin by people of Mr. Order

And called a bond of covenant by my people residing at the corner
Had established friendship to live
With the Devil my beloved Father
While other creatures do not live with him
And so they do not have me in their corridor

Thus in the whole universe it is the human being only
That lives and benefits from both of us cunningly
With Mr. Order human beings seem to fair well
With their affairs thoroughly
Similarly for me, look back for the services
 I rendered inform of wars
Those that bedeviled mankind since time immemorial
Although they suffer mostly
Some emerge with benefits and bliss finally
Because my Father with benevolent heart
Directs me to assist them kindly"

PROPHETS ARE ALWAYS RIGHT
(A dialogue between Mr. Pessimistic and Mr. Optimistic)

Mr. Pessimistic
"Who are prophets?
I fear them a lot
For making difficult moving statements
As if world is on upside down, I bet"

Mr. Optimistic
"Prophets are people of GOD
They make bold statements so hot

And predictions of what will happen in future afloat
Or interpret what happened in the past"

Mr. Pessimistic
"What if what they say
Does not happen as it is not a case before this day
Sometimes past a prophet predicted the World to end in 1984 in May
That did not happen as we are now in 2014"

Mr. Optimistic
"Prophets are always right
Even if prophesy is not fulfilled on sight
That is because either Satan has joined the fight
Or GOD time and power has no limit tight"

HYENA PRAYERS

Oh GOD! Of all creation
Why this injustice between human nation
And hyena kind your icon
By giving all animals of food to human discretion

Then you provide him with high intelligence quotient
To protect them including himself without limitation
In addition you make him eat without conditions
Both meat and plant produce from your garden

As for us you conditioned us to eat meat only alone
Using claws and teeth for catching and mastication
With little intelligence delegation
They are not enough to face human deadly weapons

Which they launch at fatal accuracy at our direction
Only the daring can endure such an onslaught devoid of compassion
How can we survive even if we have a Union?
It is a matter of time before we are swept into oblivion

GOD where have you been?
We beg you to intervene
Either you give us share of animal wealth
Or remove protection from human beings

By removing its intelligence gene
At that way he will not be keen
And we can attack his animals at noon
With no one to intervene

We can also attack him and win
Without being noticeably seen
So that we can feast of its meat at dawn
As it is compared to none

How glorious that day we win
When all weapons
Disappear including pins
Only fools will not play violins

CHAPTER IV

POLITICS

THICK SKIN

I have often heard of people talking about thick skin
They loosely use it to describe animals and human beings alike
And I have never comprehend what they mean
Am I confused?
Yes I am
Truly I know of animals with thick skin and fur
As for humans
I have never seen them with thick skin
They have the same skin thickness like any one
Yet they describe them having thick skin

Does it mean I do not know?
Observe and note their attitudes and behaviors

Especially before and after elections
They are sensitive and responsive
To people needs before elections
 And insensitive to their needs after elections

The truth of the matter is that
Animals have thick skin
To keep them warm
From rigors of cold weather
While politicians have thick skin
To keep them cold
From rigors of people's complaints

REAL PEACE COMES AFTER DEATH

In a spectrum are peace and war
War occupies one end far
Peace occupies other end near
In the middle is the cold war bar

How mistaken when middle bar is called peace
If they tell you they are there teasing
For rights are still being violated at ease
In essence it is war with weapons ceased

Do not think you have peace when there is wealth
Or when you enjoy time with your kin and kith
There is no peace as long as you sense and breathe
Real peace comes with death

IN A LION KING DEN
(The hidden agenda)

There was an urgent call
For a meeting in the Majesty palace hall
Animals were invited to attend without fail
The agenda was to design a developmental goal

Early morning the hall was full of animals
They sat in line from short to tall
And from suspicious to bold
Then the Majesty entered and there was a lull

He then asked the animals to describe the hall odor
Before he could introduce the topic proper
All the animals kept silence for a quarter of an hour
After which his Majesty asked for responses starting with the nearer

The nearest was Mr. Donkey
He described it as foul and sickly
For this, he invited wrath from his Majesty
And was hacked to death at gateway

The next was Mr. Gauzily
He called the hall sweetie
But he met the same tragedy
As Mr. Donkey for flattery

The third was Mr. Fox
He said because of common cold he could not smell well that day

This tricked his Majesty to dismiss the gathering quickly
And retired on his prey to satisfy his appetite gently

POWER SHARING
(A dialogue between Mr. Little mind and Mr. Big mind)

Mr. Little mind
"Power is too little cannot be shared
Unscrupulous can turn it like petal
 And strike back at your middle
Besides it is too beautiful like a pearl
To be shared with undeservingly idle"

Mr. Big mind
"Power is too big can be shared
Distribute fairly to those who tick
And make sure you supervise them every week
To keep in control those who tick
 And moderate those who lick"

Mr. Little mind
"Those who tick can mishandle the power cake
Which history has evolved for my sake
Besides this was my make
Those who want to partake
Cannot do it at my wake"

Mr. Big mind
"Be logical Mr. little mind
When you share instead you gain
When a mistake of any kind

Happens in line
You share blame like wine"

CRIMINAL

They call me criminal
Because of violating the laws cardinal
From the most powerful
I accept without denial

If by chance a role changes and I'm powerful
I shall watch through eyes of an owl
Push them by a power of a bull
And also brand them criminal

A criminal is a brand name
Given by the most powerful in a game
To the most socially lamed
In order to have them submissive and be tamed

DILEMMA IN HANDLING STRONG ENEMIES

If you face them headlong
That is a suicide trend
It will not be too long
Before you dangle on a hang

If you avoid them, you give them control
They have space to stroll
Leaving you to crawl
Without a role

And if you appease them, you lose your dignity
You are left with pity
As they may throw you out of the city
Before you are ready

Give them no dime
And not a chance to smear your name
As they may make you indulge in a wine
Solution is patience and time

CONFLICT

Conflict is solvable when all sides are right
They divide the cake equally from height
Each side sees the uselessness of a fight
Instead they see through darkness a light
And their future relations so bright

Conflict also disappears blank
 When all sides are wrong
No one to whom a cake belongs
They will either sing a song
Or play a game of ping pong

However when each side holds right by its tail
Conflict by and large prevails
Each side pins down its claim with a nail
In the process they produce wails
The intensity is measured by marks in the field

DIALOGUE BETWEEN MR. PEACE AND MR. WAR

Mr. Peace
"Mr. War, why do you always put people against each other?
Causing havoc and leaving death at your trail thither
Have your sympathy and compassion withered?
Don't you believe in God the Father?
What will be your destiny when the Day of Judgment gathers?"

Mr. War
"I do feed on victims
For that was the share given to me by HIM
But why do you put blame on a shadow rim?
I only come in when there is failure of your dictum
And when you change your mind at whim"

Mr. Peace
"When I try to keep peace
Selfishness and greed come to shatter it to pieces
Leaving me kneeling at my knees
Closing my eyes and longing for Almighty to ease
But they leave me praying and invite you to feast"

Mr. War
"Selfishness and greed are my nephew and niece
Do not point a blaming finger on golden geese
Lest they will catch your disease
If you do not want us interfering with your days
Then let GOD remove avarice and life pleasures"

DR. BELLARIO AHOY NGONG GENG

EFFIGY OF INJUSTICE

You alone stand lofty at ease
With your huge and majestic countenance
Dominating the neighborhood scene
Making everyone watching with awe
Yet you are nothing but an effigy of injustice

Look! People are at their knees
Hailing and praising your piece
Your servants rejoicing and displaying your keys
A show of riches and social status they tease
Yet you are nothing but an effigy of injustice

People on you lavish praise
And glorify your place
Look! Children clamoring for a chance to kiss
After playing merry-go-around to their best
Yet you are nothing but effigy of injustice

THE PRINCIPLED PERSONALITY

Look! Your body glitters bright
And your head in position upright
A virtue that makes one ticks with pride
In you we resist unbecoming pressures right
Making way for the truth to drive home with bride

That is right when you have a power role
Commanding the rest to conform to a call
Moving towards a defined goal

Nobody likes to remain nailed
When even the crippled is ahead bold

As the principled personality ticks
All his crew will follow suit
And opportunists will be less visible
Signaling rise of the moral trend in a society
As the country ascends up in value

THE UNPRINCIPLED PERSONALITY

See a figure standing at crossroad
Waiting for a wind to blow hard
Once a wind blew over a westwards road
And there he followed the direction suit
Until he reached the sea shore boat

There a wind lost its power mode
But after a moment an opposite wind came hot
And with it moved towards the eastwards port
Passed the crossroad spot
Over hanged by heavy clouds

Before stopping, a wind blew from the north
Towards the south
And there he took the southwards course
From where another wind named youth
Brought it back to the north direction close

When will he be stable lo!?
In a situation where he cannot do

Or utter a word no
Without inviting a foe
Only when he enters his grave below

MASTER OF ILL INTENTIONS

You think you are clever and fair
By hiding your ill intentions with care
When you pretend innocence like hare
To take unwary unaware

Wait for a time of taking action course
Either from duty or forced
The untold secret of your ill disposed
But hidden intentions will be exposed

As you keep your feelings hidden
Time ticks to salute your crown
They remain unknown
Until actions talk louder than a microphone

UNITY AND HYPOCRISY

Unity comes when people
Share mutual interests on the table
In a win-win situation level
When no one evokes evil

Unity disappears when people in league
Have their interests in conflict

In a win-lose situation covered with tricks
When one side mumbles and the other side clicks

In between and common is hypocrisy
People on their lips talk unity and mercy
Deep inside them they nurse conspiracy
To quench thirst of their jealousy

WHEN THEFT CEASES TO BE A CRIME

They call me Theft
This world my father left
Leaving me an orphan and in debt
Then I decided to establish the Theft web

When I was young
Only poor people joined my rank
The state outlawed our gang
And I was considered a crime

But as time passed by day
Powerful and rich joined my way
In a time split our booties filled our bay
And I ceased to be a crime by the way!

LIBERATION FROM PROBLEMS

Problems and human existence lo!
Form a team of one boat crew
Since humans were created in a zoo
Problems were created too

Problems exist as human beings exist
Efforts to liberate people from all fixes
Is chasing a crazy wind axis
What is possible is making them less crises

Problems will disappear if humans disappear
If humans do not disappear from the sphere
They will continue to haunt mankind at the rear
Forever and ever every year

CONSEQUENCES OF DEFEAT

Defeat is dispersion
Or separation of one time
A united entity
Into small uncoordinated desertions
That cannot function in unison

The parts may turn to hate
Each other mad
Blaming themselves for their role in defeat
Rendering them weaker and smaller
Until they fizzle out a bit by bit

God forbids never head for a defeat
The consequences of defeat
Are sowing of a dangerous seed
That will destroy the very seat
From which central power dwells and waits

CONSEQUENCES OF VICTORY

Victory is defeat turns upside down
In victory the central entity of power
Is not adversely affected
But it becomes stronger like a metallic coin

This will lead to new venturous projects
And if successful again in perfect
They spiral upwards in respect
For a time determined by nature's prefect

Excessive victory like excessive anything
Is dangerous to a source
 As the sweetest part of life
Is placed in the middle never in the extreme wings

DECLARED AND HIDDEN ENEMIES

On your marks! Get set and take heed!
Every human creature has enemies breed
Some are declared enemies indeed
They speak and take action against one's head
You can hear and see them like you see a pit

Some are hidden enemies under your heel
When they speak to you they kneel
Never stand out to be known like a hill
But they take action under seal
So that you can only feel

Lucky if you have declared enemies already
For you can fight face to face with ferocity
Unfortunate if you have hidden bellicosity
It strikes while you face other side without pity
In addition take care, they are the majority

YOU HAVE A REASON TO WORRY

When you are whipped by law
But for others law bows
When you sleep with hungry row
While others are having belch flow
And suffering heart burns in a row

When others have their sleep robbed
While others are having sweet hope
When you do not have a job
While others push their relatives to a top

When you are a tool for nationalism
While others are masters right
When you speculate suicide
While others with their brides
Spend honeymoons at seasides

PRINCIPLED VERSUS OPPORTUNIST

Principled persons are few scattered sparingly
They are not destined to rule generally
If they do, they fall off very quickly

They cannot join opportunists compatibly
And if they do they fail miserably
As they cannot dance to their tune amicably

Opportunists are many they can make a tower
They are destined to rule longer
They do so for a long time ever
Massing wealth and wielding power
They are prone to be dictators and murderers
For they do not have good characters

Do not lose hope Oh principled!
Even if you cannot rule for long hold
You are rare like gold
Your name cannot be tarnished at all
As for opportunists doll
Their names do not fill good books of the world

INJUSTICE IS IMMORTAL

Injustice is invincible so strong like steel
And cannot be removed like rail
In all, struggles against injustice fail
What actually changes is the master's nail
While injustice continues to prevail

Injustice passes from one master to another
Once one master is defeated on the alter
It migrates to a winning master
In addition master of injustice never
Has tribe or color

The master may be a foreign element
Or your country fellows with intent
Or maybe your family members in your den
If you do not know this fact before
Know it now before the end

ORDINARY CITIZEN DILEMMA

I want to embrace anarchy as a whole
Whereby in freedom I stroll
For whatever issue I embroil
Without anyone control

But Ah! Someone stronger
Than me can rob my properties all together
And can threaten my life if ever I temper
With his ambition to satisfy ego

But when I make a government to be
By putting some to be in charge of me
I'm made the beast of taxation fees
Any tax I must bear from head up to the knee

Indeed I'm at crossroads
I cannot move forwards
Or backwards
Up or downwards

The only alternative is to put a rope
On my neck with a hope
Of hanging myself until I drop
As both systems treat me a no body shop

When I was about to kick away
The feet support to enable the body to sway
A striking thunderbolt cut the rope mid way
And the deep voice bellowed beyond the sky

"Do not kill yourself my child, go around
You are my image well drawn
From all Earth creations I planned
Of which I'm so proud"

DIALOGUE BETWEEN MR. KNOW-HOW AND MR. INFERIORITY COMPLEX

Mr. Know-how:
"I wonder why I'm neglected and marginalized by you
While I can be of value as you know
Because of my knowledge of know-how
That can make your dreams row"

Mr. Inferiority complex:
"Your know-how is my enemy, I swear
If I allow you now
You will know my secrets raw
And use them to take my place at ago"

Mr. Know-how:
"That is not the case Mr. Inferiority complex, I vow
I shall use my know-how saw
To help you make wise decisions that draw
Attention for the good of this country under your tow"

Mr. Inferiority complex:
"Nonsense, you think I'm a fool to admit something low
I'm better off without your paws
For now I do accept what falls inside my jaws
And for what stands my way on the ground, I mow"

ORDERS AND RESULTS

Orders well planned
Bring desired results
With people happy and ululating
There is much hope triggering
Future progressive plans
Owners of orders are hailed as heroes

Orders without good plans
Bring undesired results
With people so gloomy
Regretting and lamenting
They emerge with eyes down cast
And tails stuck between their hind legs

What then will they do?
People with nurtured and tender hearts
Will never repeat the same again
But people with feeble and capricious minds
Will keep repeating bad orders
Until they dig their own graves

PHYSICAL FORCE VERSUS WISDOM

Physical force and wisdom repel each other
When sheer physical force enters a house
Invited by weakness of wisdom
To resolve a problem
Wisdom flies out of the window

But when wisdom prevails in a room
Physical force packs its luggage
And imprisons itself in a dungeon
It stays there until released and unleashed
Again by weakness of wisdom

LEADERS ARE DIFFERENT

Who says they are one
With one mind set
And one style
They are not one
They are different
But in groups

One group wants their name
To glitter while alive
They do not care losing them
When they are dead
Because they want to enjoy
The material world at any cost

The other group wants their name
To glitter now and after death
They do not mind
Sacrificing material world
For the sake of making
Their names immortal

THE MAKING OF A DICTATOR OR A DEMOCRAT

They swarm around
Laughing to every word a leader says
Even if it is non sensible
Supporting every statement with acclaim
Telling the leader and reminding him
That he is indispensable
And that he has super qualities
This in exchange of a position or fortune
These types of politicians are called opportunists
Opportunists build a dictator

The others follow a leader
With attractive principles
They revere not a leader
But his principles and objectives
And the means to achieve them
They stay around to get influenced
Make critical analysis of policies
And to participate in decision making
These types of politicians are principled
 The principled makes a democrat

DEMOCRACY AT THE BALANCE

Democracy is the rule of numbers
Whatever the larger number decides
Is what prevails
Bu if the larger number rejects
Democracy itself or its principles
Is that action democratic?

If it is democratic
Then democracy is lost
In the corridors of politicians
Better look for it with searching lamps
And strong strings to tie it when found

If it is not democratic
Then remove numbers
From the description of democracy
And describe it on the bases
Of principles only

Thus democracy will be the rule of virtues
Of fairness, transparency, faithfulness
And trustworthiness etc., without numbers
Thus even if an issue is decided by numbers
It is still undemocratic unless it embodies the virtues

POLITICS ARE COMPLICATED

Politics are complicated
Because of two types of conflicting interests

DR. BELLARIO AHOY NGONG GENG

Subjective interest, serving selfish desires
Objective interest, serving public needs

In the process the forces of objective interests
Give way to the forces of subjective interests
As they are stronger
And the country goes down the drain

However in very rare circumstances
The forces of public interests prevail
And the country goes up the ladder
Of peace and progress

The complicated part of it is that
Those pursuing selfish interests
Do say that they are pursuing public interests
Is it not hypocrisy to the highest degree?

HANDS OF A LEADER

A leader has two hands
A soft one made of spongy material
He tenderly pushes people towards a goal
And a heavy hand made of metallic material
He uses an iron fist to drive issues
Towards the direction of his interest
Whether people like it or not

His fade depends
On how he uses the two hands
Vis-à-vis the foreign and internal issues

If he uses a soft hand on foreign affairs
And a heavy one on internal affairs
He reduces to a selfish dictator
En route to fade out in history

But if he uses a heavy hand
On foreign affairs
And a soft hand on his people
He will be hailed a hero
And live so long after his death
As one generation carries his name
And passes it to the other generations

FEELING INSECURE

He is anxious and emotional
Jumping up and down
Devouring everywhere with his eyes
And suspecting every spot
Definitely he is feeling insecure

But those maneuvers will not help him
Instead he may head to another insecure situation
As they are everywhere available and spread like stars
As for secured places they are few and far like planets
Only the wise and the composed can get them

Never try to control fire with a bare hand
Or balance a tight string with shaky feet
As you can sustain a burned hand
Or get a foot slip
With your whole body tumbling down

But what can he do while he is in this danger?
Where all carnivores are surrounding him
And birds of prey
Are hovering at a close distance
It is a matter of time before they consume him

But he cannot help by spreading
His feet and hands aimlessly about
He can be safe if he composes
Start on his marks, gets set and goes
After receiving valuable technical advice

Remember the good advice
Cannot come passively
But must be actively sought from the sages
They are too thrifty to give away
Their invaluable property without demand

WAR AGAINST INJUSTICE

In a war against Injustice
Do not fight those who make Injustice
For they will react fighting you
Diverting you away from fighting
The real enemy the Injustice
If you want to fight
Fight Injustice itself

But how do you do it?
Fighting the abstract?
Yes, you can fight the abstract

And the good part of it is that
You are assisted in a fight
By even the perpetrators themselves
Since you are not directing your swords against them
But against the isolated beast the Injustice
And who can stand supporting Injustice?
As it is hated by all including those who use it
Provided that they are not identified with it

Fight Injustice by exposing its front and back
Fight its effect on every one including the perpetrators
Using the tool of education without mentioning any name
You will be surprised!
Everyone with no exception will fight it
By enacting laws and by changing the life styles
If you want to know as to who did it before
As every good technique has a precedent
Contact the work of Gandhi
And Martin Luther King junior
You will never hesitate a minute

COUNTRY

You country with silver platted borders
Inhabited by people who have experienced horror
You want to develop, progress and happy?
No way, your fate is by chance daddy

Whereby the majority of the unscrupulous guys
Take affairs of your state between your eyes
And driving you into the swarm of lice

Rarely could a scrupulous hand run you
Because they are few like rare animals in a zoo
Like gold they can rust not
In fact they are like God

But people change the name
By adding letter "l" between "o" and "d"
To make them not quarrel with God
What else can they do?

TWO BIRTHS OF A NATION

One birth by its citizens
As they fight against foreign domination
And for freedom of their hands and minds
Blood, tears and sweat flow profusely
To secure these virtues

Another by its leader
Establishing durable systems
And seeing them done
By him and others while alive

How happy that country will be
Harmony, peace, unity and prosperity
Will have a sanctuary to live
As they have these times been displaced
And rendered destitute
Citizens will look back with pride
And look ahead with hope
As they transcend times and epochs
Truly limitless sky is the limit

ENTERING DARKNESS AND VICE VERSA

When entering darkness, by all account you don't know
But wait a minute!
Only those standing by and gazing
At your ordeal can see you entering darkness
Haven't you once looked at a dying person
Entering darkness in peace while relatives wail?

As for entering the light
You can clearly see after an initial shock
Don't you see a born child gasping for air?
And crying caused by irritation made by light?
Is nature not fair and consistent?

In the same vein entering political darkness
Is never conceived by the subjects
But the standbys do
At the final scenario
The standbys fill the vacuum
As nature loathes vacuum

INJUSTICE IN FRANK DISCOURSE

I wonder why what people say is not what they do
In public people cry out to the top of their voices
To have me strangled, killed and buried
But when I'm to be killed
Some people from all classes of the society
Release me and beg me
To do important services to them

Thus the powerful need me
As a tool to settle scores with their opponents
The middle class want me to increase their wealth
To become more powerful
Some poor need me to dispossess another poor
So that they can survive

Since they are weak to take from the powerful classes
This I do on their request
I have never done anything without orders from them
But after I have finished the job
And when I wanted to go for a walk and leisure
The same people bark and howl on sighting me
Wishing me to hang and dangle on a post
How pretentious they are!

ALMIGHTY IS NOT MEDIOCRE

Look and observe what he is doing
Is he on his proper sense?
Or are we mediocre?
Look! With the grace of his two hands
He is using one hand to extinguish fire
And with other he rekindles fire

Definitely we are mediocre
Since we do not understand this riddle
His friend told me he does that
To prevent fire from wrecking havoc at one hand
And from disappearing completely on the other
As it was his duty to keep fire and use it wisely

By doing that he is stuck in a rut
Never moving forward or backward
Until Almighty relieves him from burden
And blaming him for wasting time
By not performing the mission bestowed upon him
Will he be given another? I doubt, Almighty is not mediocre

UNCOVERING THE VILE

I did not know
Believe me I did not know
Parents taught me
But it was not available
In their curriculum
Teachers took me over
Again it was not in their syllabuses

But when I joined the school of politics
To my surprise
I found it in abundance
It is when one pretends
To work with someone he does not want
And it is when one welcomes with a smile
A person he would like to chop to pieces

They say this is the art of politics
Deceiving the unwary
In order to prevail at the top
Those who practice it survive longer
Those who do not lose out quickly
Poor are the people
They deserve pity in abundance

DR. BELLARIO AHOY NGONG GENG

WHETHER TO SUPPORT A CAUSE OR NOT

Do you want to support a cause?
Do not depend on aims alone
Although aims are important
But also consider the means
Used to reach the aims

If means are plausible and humane
Then support it
Otherwise stay away and search for other means
Never heed to the Machiavellian adage
"Means justify the end"

Crooked and inhumane means
Are like shortest cuts to a destination
They make one reach the aim quiet easily
While humane means are long and tortuous
One has to sweat much to get to a goal

Inhumane means present
A short cut at the beginning
At the end they lead to doom
Better adopt the humane means
As they justify the good end

WHEN WRONG BECOMES RIGHT

Do not tread that road
Do not follow that road
That road is for Mr. Right

Only he who can walk that road
Only he who can live in that mansion

But who are you to prevent me taking that road
Don't you see the person behind me with a big club?
When I'm with that giant
I cease to be called Mr. Wrong
For I have automatically changed from wrong to right
From now on
You revise the lessons you took years back
And note the equation
Power plus Wrong
Can change Wrong to Right
And wrong many times repeated can be right

YOU WILL BE HISTORY YOURSELF

Left alone you destroy
Assisted you don't like
What do you want?
This is a behavior of a child
But a child has small body
And a small brain
As for you
You have a big body and a big brain
Better learn from history
In order to forge ahead
Failure to do so
You will be history your self

DR. BELLARIO AHOY NGONG GENG

FRIENDSHIP AND POLITICS

Politics mix with friendship
Blinds eyes and deafens ears
The Authority becomes blind and deaf
It will never see and hear from others
In fact it is deaf alive in politics
Waiting to be buried in its grave

But no my friend
Its friends can be its ears and eyes
It will speak of something it has not heard
And sign anything it has not understood
While continuing warming
The political seat

If that is so, then we are in for an ordeal
In a political voyage
Where friends become the real rulers
Without mandate from the public
What is the remedy? Do we have one?
We are stuck like a rat in a rut

FIGHTING THE LION'S SHADOW

He met a lion at the green valley
The lion had an aggressive mood
It was hungry for it has stayed
Many days without food
By instinct he gave it a chunk of meat
He had acquired from hunting

Caught by fear, he began
To hit the shadow of a lion
Thinking that he would kill it
As the shadow grew shorter at mid day
He thought he had killed the lion
And began pulling away
The remaining pieces of meat
The lion filled the air with a deafening roar
And charged towards the man

The man stood motionless with fear
He cannot move forward or backward
Left side or right side
What will happen?
He will be food himself
To silence the hungry and noisy
Grinding machine of the beast stomach

SECURITY

Security, Security, Security
You always cry out for me to prevail
But when I come in my two forms;
Physical and economic
Still you are not satisfied
You keep on demanding more
What do you want exactly?
Are you in your right mind?

Even if you come with your two forms
You will not meet my aspirations

DR. BELLARIO AHOY NGONG GENG

A person does not live on those alone
But takes it in a cocktail with freedom
Without freedom
Your physical and economic security
Will be like taking a meal
Without salt and spices

You want me to come with freedom?
That is too much you are demanding
How shall I enjoy the economic security?
In presence of freedom with roving eyes
I tell you one thing my friend
I cannot self inflict the feet I walk with
If you do not want me without freedom
Then go to hell, I'm not coming

MOVING TOWARDS A BOTTOMLESS PIT

Some think they are moving forward
By taking one step forward
And one step backward
They think, they will deceive the unwary
For seeing them moving

But in fact they are deceiving themselves
For very soon, many will notice
They are standing akimbo in one place

Three ways; forward and two sides
 Are blocked with barricades

The only accessible is backward movement
Tracing back without turning the face backward
Because they have been restricted by a narrow alley

Look! There is a pit in the middle of the alley
By God it is fathomless!
How will they survive?

LIGHT WHERE ARE YOU?

Light where are you?
We know bats hate you
That is why they hide
From you during a day
And domestic flies love you
That is why they swarm around
Enjoying your rays
As you traverse the skies

But these days you are not found
Leaving bats to love and to merry making
This is unfair of you
God created you and darkness
-To interchange
So that creatures in love with each one
Can enjoy them selves

We are sinking deeper with darkness
God knows whether we shall survive
As we cannot go about our life businesses
But wait a deep divine voice is cautioning us

Not to get worried
For when it is the darkest
The stars pop out with abundant light
To that, our hearts rest with hope

WHEN FROGS SUDDENLY STOP CROAKING

When frogs suddenly stop croaking
There is something passing by
Maybe looking for them to harm
They hide for their lives
Danger passing out
They start to croak again

When people stop talking
There is looming danger around them
Passing by, they resume talking again
But when it persists, unlike the frogs
They loudly talk not with their tongues
But with their weapons

There is a danger in audible sound waves
Whether from animals or people
Because they expose them to danger
They also warn them of the danger
In that way, they are double edged swords

PRISON WALL OF HUMAN BEINGS

Unlike the usual stone wall
Of prison which has no senses
The prison wall of human beings
Have ears, nose and eyes
In that way it is deadly to the prisoner

The prisoner never hears, smells or sees
On release, he is either dead
 En route to the grave yard
 Or alive with sensations numb

But many people love the prison wall of human beings
They make them standout tall
And great among the other citizens
How do you say this has a drastic effect on them?
While they are enjoying it
They fight hard to remain in prison

Oh! But they are not human beings any longer
They are deformed by prison beyond recognition
As they have become devil incarnate
Do you want to be like them?
No sir, I better languish in my own state
Sanctioned by the Creator

GRID SYSTEM IN TURMOIL

Grid system is in normal operation
When it separates

DR. BELLARIO AHOY NGONG GENG

Wanted from unwanted
Or wanted but categorized
Into different sizes and shapes

It is an abnormal operation
When both wanted or unwanted
Pass through it
In that way such a grid
Will never be useful again

You seem to be driving us through science
Let us apply that knowledge to politics
Does governance have a grid system?
Yes it has
In fact they have many types

The most important
Is the personal loyalty grid
It separates those
Not loyal and principled
From those loyal and opportunistic

When things are good
The loyal and opportunistic
Kiss the master's cheeks
And when things turn bad
They kick the master's butts

Not loyal and principled
Remain steadfast
In all those changes
Like water current in a giant river
It will never be fast or slow

JACK OF TWO TRADES

Believe me Dad
Last night, I had a dream
It was a nightmare
I saw a human being at a distance
He was so handsome
I had never seen such a lad before
He was of normal height
Well balanced body proportions
Quite logical and articulate
In presenting issues

By God he is a Nationalist!
Observe his speech
He talks about a fair
Distribution of a national cake
And how evil the corruption is

When I came nearer, his demeanor changed
The face became longer with oblong head
He became shorter and walked on four legs
His speech was a stutter
And was relieving employees
From their salaries at pen point
Not satisfied he would straddle the street
And relieve peoples' pockets at knife point
This scenario is incredible
How can he be two in one?

CHASING WINDS

Do not chase winds
In an attempt to catch them
Today they are enemies
Tomorrow they are friends
In between they leave fans
Gracing martyrdom

Then they dance in a whirlpool
And sink into the bottom of an ocean
To resurface again before
They swim to the shore
As for you, you go up and down with tide

Until you take in enough and get drowned
At last you end up in
An ocean beast belly
Or in a martyr tomb
Viva martyr day!

WOLF IN A SHEEP CLOTH

Look at that animal coming
See the head, the ears and the eyes
By God it is a sheep in every aspect
Even the voice mimics
Exactly the sheep kind

But when you come closer and scan the details
Another kind of animal emerges

Spotted skin body lies under the sheep skin
And long ears of a real animal
Were covered by a skin of a sheep ear
And real brown eyes were covered
By an artificial sheep eyes
By God, it is a wolf!

It is coming towards the real sheep kraal
There is a danger to these animals
How can it be detected? While the owner is blind
And deaf at the same time
It is coming nearer to the owner
Look, he is touching its skin from behind to the head
Satisfied, he allowed it to enter the kraal
What will come to their protection? Only GOD knows

SEARCH FOR HIS MAJESTY THE FREEDOM

They walked, ran and hid
Away from cruelty of injustice
And daringly walking
Towards the abode of freedom
For three weeks they searched
Slept in the bush with wild animals
Ate wild food to prevent starvation
And drank urine of colleagues
To quench thirst

Then at last they heard his Majesty
Sweet voice beckoning them
They yelled, ululated, danced and giggled

Despair retreated before hope
And injustice stuck its tail
Between its hind legs
Rag clothes were thrown away
Tyre shoes were discarded
And hair shaved and combed

But alas! A giant Monster
A former Injustice incarnate
Appeared again from the blue
And with a giant whip
Made of an animal skin
Gave freedom a severe strokes of lashes
Mainly in his back and face
He had to crawl
And pleaded with no avail
People looked on helplessly

Satisfied the Monster left him with bruises
And deep cut wounds at the face
That later healed leaving ugly scars
Defaced freedom entered the hole
To hide from shame
They kept calling his Majestic name
However with a faint coarse voice
He responded asking them to leave him alone
 As he was not worthy of the title and name

PERCEPTION OF INJUSTICE

It fell with a resounding thud on his shoulders
He thought he was hit by someone
But alas it advanced to strangle him
And put its long pair of antennae
Unto his two nostrils
To suffocate and make his life a dream
But he struggled

Eyes were engorged with blood
And sweat swallowed
Him up to his feet
Wallowing back and forth
He was able to shake injustice away
And took hold of its antennae
Holding both chin and head to twist its neck

Sensing danger injustice pleaded for its life
And requested to have
A covenant of non-aggression
Provides that he holds it
Once again on his shoulders
And throw it overboard on to the shoulders
Of another one standing across the river

The guy hesitated for its weight was unbearable
But when he wanted to give a trial
He found, it was as light as a feather
On throwing it over he was amused
Both by the easy way it left his hand
And by the heavy weight it fell on the new target
The new person felt as if hit by a giant stone

There, is learned an unforgettable lesson
One is sensitive to injustice done to him
But quite unaware
Of injustice he does to others
Few who are aware, if they exist
Are Gods incarnate

CONSEQUENCES OF POWER AND WEAKNESS

Beyond the clouds on the horizon arose a gigantic figure
His body that of an elephant and body muscles corrugated
To look like that of a boxer or a wrestler
On the opposite horizon appeared seven strong youth
Brandishing their swords and threatening to cut the giant into pieces
At the zenith appeared also seven mixed group of all ages and sexes
Moving towards the giant with joyous choirs
To them the giant was their protector

From the East walking bare foot are seven guys
They are tired, exhausted from a walk and hunger
They are being followed by a swarm
Of eagles and vultures
Those have gathered to rescue their meat
Surprisingly no hope for their rescue
As they do not have sympathizers

Nature is strange and funny in deed
When a person or an organized group is powerful
They have many enemies and many friends

But when they are weak or poor
They have many enemies and no friends
Perhaps their friend is mother nature her self
It just welcomes them to her bosom
Since it has no hands to fight

SERVITUDE AND FREEDOM

When conditions connive and push one to servitude
There, there is pain, sweat and gnashing of teeth
At the end dignity and self worth are lost
One longs to get away from it
To the promised land of freedom
Where lodges dignity and self worth
Pain and suffering are damned in the dustbin of history

But on the way to freedom and beyond
Exist hills and mountains to be surmounted
And to be overcome through sweat and pain
At the end one survives either by passing
Through a hole of a needle or fall dead
As if providence told them to chose
Between servitude and death

This is strange, queer and mind boggling
It is like being caught between two lethal foes
But wait and think before making an erroneous conclusion
It is true, freedom and servitude all have prices to be paid
But you only pay a price of death when seeking freedom
And pay a huge one with dignity when in servitude
Which do you prefer?

DR. BELLARIO AHOY NGONG GENG

NEED FOR CHANGE

I heard them talk
Some words were audible
And some were whisperings
I had to streamline my ears to eavesdrop them
One said there was no need for a change, any change
Since people he were serving are happy with him
Another said there was need for change
For the reason that even though popular
There must be a very tiny, tiny minority
Those are writhing under one's weight
They are suffering, straining and sweating
While one does not know or feel

But the other voice
For no change retorted
Those are a very small minority
And so what if they strain
That minority will never count
More over this is what democracy requires

The voice for Change asserted that
They all love Democracy
But those minorities are human
And they have human rights
Enshrined in the constitutions of all
Civilized and democratic nations
Democracy does not allow
Human life to suffer
And so there is need for change
I sensed them coming towards my direction

And so I absconded and disappeared
Without their notice

LAMENT OF MY COUNTRY

From my children, my own children
At home I keep feeding them
Sometimes with milk and honey
And sometimes with cocktails
Of drinks and food
When finances are tight
I feed them with concoctions of austerity

Every day they make me a loo
And deposit on me their waste
That lot I would take down my belly
Wash myself with detergents
And wait for another deposit to come

Not happy with all that service
Some continued to suck me dry
I'm now left with skin on bones
And internal vital organs
Very soon these organs will shrink
And seize to function
Thrusting my life in a dustbin of history

MISSING A TARGET

On a National day
A play was concocted
To consummate the occasion
Two pairs of opposites were matched
And contesters were asked to identify
And fight the most undesirable enemy
One contester boasted he knew
The enemies of human kind

At first Ignorance appeared with Knowledge
He lunged forward and fought the Knowledge
Then came Poor performance and Good performance
He welded his sword and beheaded Good performance
After came Corruption and Integrity
He suffocated Integrity leaving Corruption amused
At last came Disorder and Order
He gave Order a blow, throwing away what it ate in a vomit
Other contesters never attempted
-And disappeared in horror
At the end of a game the winners were
Ignorance, Poor performance, Corruption and Disorder
They were decorated with gold medals
Leaving people asking questions in bewilderment
How did he miss the target?
Does he know the real enemies?

WE ARE IN A BOAT

We are in a boat
One boat
Being steered by a crew
One crew
And boarded by people
One people
The boat tosses to
One direction
Then to the other
One side
At last it stood in the middle
At once
Neither moving forward
One step
Nor moving backward
One inch
Neither did the crew ask for help
One time
Nor did they ask people for assistance
One moment
At the end rescue came from one
One God
Because the final destination is one
To one Creator

DR. BELLARIO AHOY NGONG GENG

BETWEEN SLEEP AND AWAKE

Be between sleep and awake
And you will understand
The meaning of the word uncomfortable

Be between sleep and awake
And you will understand
The meaning of the word undesirable

Be between sleep and awake
And you will understand
The meaning of the word distasteful

Be between sleep and awake
And you will understand
The meaning of the word unbearable

Be between sleep and awake
And you will understand
The meaning of the word unpalatable

Do not let your country slip
Into between sleep and awake
For you will experience all of the above

If it is forced to do that
You better pull it out quickly into full awake
By showering it with cold water

Or otherwise let it sleep completely
Never to get awake
For nature hates continuous suffering

MR. KNOWLEDGE AND MR. POWER

The gentlemen on stage are two
One is called Mr. Knowledge
Handsome with eagle eyes
And the other Mr. Power
Huge with roving eyes

When they are combined together
The taste of their cocktail blend
Depends on the amount of knowledge
A person has
Adequate, he will be humbled, prudent and wise
Little, he is intoxicated, rude and oppressive

Adequate knowledge and power combined
Are blessed and humane
Future of humans depend on it
Little knowledge and power combined
Is a curse just like wild fire is

DOUBLE PERSONALITY

Walking with self confidence unprecedented
He has graduated from two schools
One teaching Mr. Fox style curriculum
And the other the King Lion style
From the Royal college

Meeting a strong rival
He would use a Fox style

To avoid danger as there will be fierce reaction
He would even accommodate him in his den
And nourishes him with pretended smiles

And meeting a weak enemy he would use a Lion style
Since he would kill it without sustaining struggling wounds
And reverting to Fox style
He would then weep over the body of his victim
Play innocence to impress the relatives
And assist in burying the dead

This tactic is time bound
For when both enemies
Learn from the School of Occidental Studies
He will not play a role of a Fox and a Lion again
As Fox brain will be removed and Lion claws extracted
Believe me or not that double personality will split asunder

KIDNAPPED

On a voyage in a boat
They sailed for three weeks
Amid the storm
Finally they saw the shore
At a sudden one of them in a boat
Jumped on the Captain's neck
And had him drowned

The assailant then in control
Instead of using his hands to steer a boat
Turned his head upside down

And pressed his eyes
At the bottom of the boat
And rowed the boat with his two legs
One on each side of the boat

Suddenly the boat veered
Away from the shore
No one knows where they are heading to
Nature has two options
Either to press them against its bosom
Or produce a miracle
There is no other course

A HOUSE ON A HEAP OF SAND

A house built on a heap of sand
Cannot endure and stand
As foundation is on a shaky ground
Where are cement and wire bands?
The inhabitants will be in a danger van
Condemned to death before hand

But who are you to tell me this?
Leave me alone
For I'm confused now
How can you say this?
While I was told by experts
That it is worthwhile to build on sand
Because it is clean and does not make water to clog

You are in for duping my friend
They tell you this so that your house collapses
Your instinct should find truth
Among plethora of false advice
Otherwise they will mock at you
When your house is in rubble
And you will mourn and regret
If ever you survive

TAKING RIGHT AND WRONG DECISIONS

Taking right or wrong decision
Depends on targets and strategies
If targets and strategies are plausible
Decisions will be right

If targets and strategies are imperfect
Decisions will be wrong
Those affected will grumble and burn in rage
Swearing to grill the perpetrators in a furnace

On discerning, the perpetrators
Stick their tails behind the legs
And seek protection in a wall
Made of armed guards

A TREE WITH WEAK ROOTS

A tree anchored by vertical roots
And supported by horizontal ones

Lives longer and resists
The pressure of nature
The vertical roots sink deeper
In search of water and nutrients
How deep they may be
Is this not a blessing?

But a tree
With only the horizontal roots
Supported by tendrils
Cannot withstand pressures
As it is malnourished and weak
Its doom is predicted
Circumscribed and known
Before its day

Beware oh planter!
As you plant to make a forest
For future generation
Select those species with roots
That has strong soil penetrating power
Otherwise you will weep and regret
When a wind like Haiyana comes
And erases that giant forest down at a swoop

FIGHTING FOR FREEDOM

Freedom is fought by all
But felt and enjoyed by few
The few keep telling the majority
That they are free

They keep repeating it
And enforcing it

Until people too
Think they are free
Because they see it
A distance far glittering
But when they go there
They do not get it

Is freedom a mirage?
To majority, yes
But to the few, no
Because they really live it
And enjoy it
As it is so sweet

WAR AND PEACE

When friends disagree
And enemies agree
You are at war
You are at peace
When friends agree
And enemies disagree

Keep friendship like a pearl
For with it is bound
The fate of peace and war
Tie enmity with a string of steel
So taut never to get loose a little
To prevent it to steal secrets hidden in a motel

Do not allow both your friends and enemies to agree
When that happens your days are counted on earth
As both of them know your weaknesses and strengths
Definitely they will hit at weak points
Leaving you cursing life and the Creator

Here is a trick
Better enter a grave
With a name engraved on the top
They will stop pursuing you
As they fear very much the grave

THE GREATEST LEADER

The greatest leader is the one who appeals
To opponents while keeping
The loyalty of the supporters
He appeals to conscience rather than interest
In other words he is tall in the crowd

The weakest leader is the one who appeals
To his supporters only
Keeping his opponents at bay
He appeals to interest rather than to conscience
In other words he is a dwarf in the crowd

The choice is absolutely yours
If you want enduring peace and unity
Follow the tall leader
And if you want continuous war and strife
Follow the dwarf leader

FACING LIFE CHALLENGES

Facing life challenges
One has to fight war in two fronts
One internal and the other external
The internal war is to crush
The resistance of one's fellow mates
They too have an axe to grind with him
For they do not want him
To bypass them and be important

After overcoming the internal fight
At his door step is the external war
They want him crushed so as to get their fortunes
If he resists them, he is a hero among his fellows
But if he loses he will wet the appetite
Among his fellow mates
They will then strike him down
And sit on the throne

Life is a struggle
Between two forces
The forces of survival
And the forces of doom
At the end the forces of survival
Succumb to the forces of doom
Here is a valid conclusion
Life is by and large chasing of wind

WHEN THINGS FALL APART OR PULL CLOSE

When a boss has a heart of steel
And a mind of stone
Things fall apart
Like a live body deficient of life needs
People under that boss will suffer
And so they disown a leader

But when a boss has a heart of flesh
And a mind made up of a network of nerves
Things pull close
Like a live body well nourished and full of vitality
The people will surround and offer defense
And ready to die with him

Never wear a steel heart
Or a stony mind
If you want to survive long enough
For people will use the steel to dig your grave
And use the stone to fill the grave
What do you gain?

DICTATORSHIP

I thought you were a an abstract
But when I met you
I now know you are real
For when you are being used by me
I love you
To extent I never want to leave you
 Until we are separated by a grave

But if you are being used
By others
I hate you to extent
Of tearing you into pieces
Given the opportunity
This is because with you
 I do not share power with any body

My power is absolute
For nobody will dare to question me
I push those around me like buttons
To do what I want
Do you think they dislike it?
No, they like it
Because they enjoy personal gains

With disgust
I hate democracy, your opposite
For imposing on me people to share power with
By God the so call democracy is crazy
How does he tell me to share power?
While God, the Creator himself
Does not share power with any body

Recall the war he fought with Lucifer
The head of his Angels
When Lucifer wanted to share power with him
Recall also the punishmentHE gave Adam and Eve
When they committed the cardinal sin
Intended to share power with HIM

If GOD does not love democracy
Who am 'I the little creature to love it?
If I do, I shall be working against
The Almighty, the Creator
And who is that foolish
To work against the Creator?
If he is not looking for the second cardinal sin!

DEMOCRACY AND EDUCATION

Democracy cannot flourish
In an ignorant and poor society
Because ignorance and poverty
Will be used by small and canny elites
To sway away votes
Appealing to ethnicity and conditions

Democracy can flourish
In an educated and rich society
As votes will be cast
In support of public programs
Free of any intimidation

It will be after the rise
Of elite proportion of the population
To a reasonable level
Accompanied with economic well being
That democracy will have a place
To live and grow

DR. BELLARIO AHOY NGONG GENG

ROADS TO THE END CITY

You wonder which road to take
Both roads lead to END city
But poverty road makes a short cut
While comfort one takes a long walk
The struggle is whether to take a long
Or short cut

By nature of things
Many people take a short cut
Because though full of thorns
It is straight and does not need
A lot of efforts

Only few people take a long detour
The dogma of the survival
Of the fittest operates here
They go through that long road
By pushing some people to the short one

THE GREATEST FOLLY

The greatest folly
Is to work against
Oneself unaware
The price is one own gloom
En route to doom

But how can one work against oneself?
And even unaware

Unless he is a fool
Swimming in a pool
A few liters of water full

No sir, one can work against himself
When he has no knowledge
Of the consequences of his actions
He does not exert efforts
To know them before taking action

After knowing by trial and error
He will panic
Vomit and drink back his vomits
Is this not the greatest folly?
Yes it is

CHAPTER V

MISCELLANEOUS

WORLD IS FOR GOOD MANAGERS

One may be a beggar
With feet infested with jiggers
Or a criminal with daggers
Extorting to get away with loot
World is for good managers

One may be a rich merchant
Acquiring wealth to satisfy his want
Or a powerful person with gun
Using garrisons to conquer lands
World is for good managers

One may be a person of faith
Urging people to understand myths

Exhorting faithful not to fear death
And telling people to moderate earthly tastes
World is for good managers

AT CROSS ROADS, WHAT DO I DO?

I went to direction north, closed
I went to direction south, closed
I went to east coast, closed
I thought west was worth it, closed
What do I do? Who knows?

Like a victim of a ghost seized
I squatted and put my head between knees
And waited to be locked in with keys
Never dreamt to be released
What do I do?

Wonder what the next turn is
Since my best ideas are burned
I prayed to the Almighty asking for concern
And show me the way to learn
What do I do?

ARTISTS

How wonderful you are?
To the universe you imagine far
Until you bring the galaxies near
Pierce deep with your eyes and ears

To your disappointment you roll tears
How wonderful you are?
Nature you penetrate deep
Beyond the sky you dare peep
With desire to have knowledge reap
Causing human spirit to lift

How wonderful you are?
Reality you extend to infinity
Where lodges trinity
Around your vicinity
You merge nature and mind to uplift dignity

SELF EMPLOYED

Icon of freedom you are
As your toil and sweat has made you dear
You do not depend on anyone far or near
And you express your ideas without favor or fear

Intelligence you excel
As you think from what you feel
And imagine what you want
Before the results yield

In management you are good
As you control your mood
Tread rude with boot
And extravagance you shoot

DR. BELLARIO AHOY NGONG GENG

MANAGEMENT

Because of your short stature
Your importance as master sir
Cannot be noticed faster
You need to support your height on a corner
So as to fall in order

You are the common factor
If ever they want to prosper
They must pass through your sector
And if they want to use your tractor
They must do through your order

You are the common denominator
If they want a drink of a tusker
They must kiss your counter
And if to the grave they retire
They must pass your bridge over

A DISH OF WAL WAL

Dough of cereal flour
Rolled into balls for half an hour
And fried in a pan until it acquires brown color
Shall provide a dish which you can boast forever

Even if you are thirsty
And over the day fasting
You will find it refreshingly tasty
And satisfactorily long lasting

Its ingredients are many
Try first with honey
And you will report to mummy
That your day was funny

POETRY

Residing at your neighborhood is a dream
If you were among foods, you would be a cream
And if you were for building, you would be a frame
Were you to be a drink, you would fill to a brim

You make human imagination satisfied
You render some ideas mystified
While others you testified
As you hold criticism glorified

You are but pregnant
With ideas which you can't
Express as you want
As you will be a subject for a hunt

ALCOHOLISM

Together with life you are an ancient
From nothing you make a person giant
And you keep lifting him to a level short of a saint
On the ground a person sways left and right
Before sending him to orient

On humans your death tolls are in billions
On conservative side it is in millions
Yet they do not send you to Mount Zion
For you numb their senses not to know their ruin

Tricky are your tactics
At first you make a person active
Then you make him in effective
On the way to make him finally inactive

EDUCATED AND NON EDUCATED

Educated and non educated both learn
But one learns on easy way turn
Through education he earns
The other through experience burns
If he survives he will get scars from wounds

Educated on the desk travels far
He can know about war
Only falling on ears
And can learn about the creature rare
That has not been brought near

None educated travels bearing the rigors himself
He risks becoming deaf
With no one to help
And with temperatures high, he is near to melt
Recalling back the luxurious life he left

THINGS TO PRAY AND NOT TO PRAY FOR

Pray for luck to knock your door marching
As it always stays in a swamp so murky
But do not pray to be unlucky
For it always stays with you sucking

Pray to get a job
For getting it is like walking a tight rope
Do not pray to head a jobless list top
As it is always around strangling hope

Pray to be happy in the world
For it is expensive as gold
And do not pray to be unhappy lad
For it is so much around like the common cold

APPRECIATION OF THINGS FROM DISTANCE

If you want to like something fondly hard
Be at a distance far
Where details are dire
Everything looks smooth with no tear

If you want to know something clearer
Be at a distance nearer
Where details can be described better
And references can be made further

If you want to dislike something at instance
Come nearer to a touch distance

Where details are magnified by lens
And tiny crabs become giants

CULTURE

Welcome along Oh Culture!
And let us display a twist dance for an hour
To mark your birth day with pleasure
For without you society has no future

Under your motherhood
You gave society roots, food and boots
The result she was in good mood
With pride she was clad with lovely suits

You are the source of civilization smiles
Because you gave her feet to walk for miles
And tools to make roof tiles
In order to tame wild

A SATISFACTORY JOB

A satisfactory job is the one
You enjoy doing it with fun
Wishing the time not to end
And not feeling bored even when done

A satisfactory job is the one
One feels contributing to human gains
Able to contribute to posterity a coin
And feel proud to identify with John

A satisfactory job is the one
Appropriately rewarded with yen
Not triggering family happiness in vain
And helping oneself and next of kin

WHAT A DILEMMA?

Difficult to ascend a mountain
Without throwing up a complaint
But easy to come down a plain
Without experiencing pain

Difficult to get riches and power
As they have to be acquired by a sower
But easy to lose them in an hour
When they are not managed by a knower

Difficult to get a good partner in life
That will sustain love alive
But easy to get who shatters it to five
Never allow a trace to survive

MY FOLKLORE DANCE

Hear a big drum sounding loudly
And another small one in tally
All full of rhythm and melody
So sweet and tingling to nerves and body

I see youth in a hurry preparing well
The boys tethering the last cows as they kneel

The girls preparing the night meal
And getting ready to a dance zeal

"Abuk you are too slow"
Says a big brother with a voice hollow
Waiting to accompany her through a foot path narrow
To a dancing ground near the direction of a river flow

They find people already dancing to a tune
And others are on a date with friends alone
How beautiful the scenery under a moon
I regret missing folklore dances, my own

UNIVERSITY

University you are one in diversity
All knowledge converge in you mighty
You are appreciated when you produce Betty
To swell a class of witty

At all times you are double-edged like a sword
At one edge you are wise and move knowledge forward
At the other you can move the country windward
Especially when you see a country moving downward

Remember you are the light of people you lead
When light is too bright it blinds the eyes of whom you meet
And when it is too dim it makes bland a mind you need
The way out is not to be too bright or too dim in deed

ROAD

You are not only a facility for a cruiser
But absolutely a necessary Manager
In making people pass hither and thither
From one place to another

Without you villages and towns whine
For being disconnected at length
Development and trade will stop in essence
And life will fizzle out of existence

Your history matches that of animal kind
At first you are made of repeated footsteps in line
Later on your importance necessitated human kind
To make you smooth, wider and easy to find

MUSIC

Under your inviting sound
That tingle all the body around
Sensible creatures dance to your tune
Even if dances vary inform and amount

Hearts and soul are lifted up right
Requesting purification and cleansing rite
King of happiness and colorful light
Your reign has no beginning and no end in sight

If you disappear from the World scene
Happiness will follow your return

Gloom and grim will cover the earth again
Inviting darkness to reign

RAT AND ALCOHOL

I'm called rat
My staunch enemy is cat
Because it likes my meat
Its presence makes me mad

One time I was with my friend alcohol
And I felt my bravery beeped up bold
I resolved to fight the cat until yielding a soul
And drag it by whiskers hold

But alas! When I was near
And about to hold it by whiskers
Alcohol, my friend escaped leaving me with Mr. Fear
Only my legs and a hole saved my ears

SPOON

You provide leverage for taking food
Between dish and mouth port
Without you people use their hands a lot
Bearing pain of food cold and hot
Chasing away appetite and mood

In all account you are a hygienic tool
Without you people get germs as a rule

That affects body and soul
And renders it staggering like a fool
Using a spoon to empty a pool

With you one is civil
Two steps ahead of a cave level
And one step ahead of village people
Without you one is uncivil
Only a thin line separates one with an animal

PLATE

They call me eating plate
In me you take your meal even at late
Eating together with whom you relate
Leaving me empty and light to rotate

Without me you contort and squirm
Looking for anything to use at whim
This is a situation so grim
Take care; you may miss your cream

The first article you acquire at birth
And always have it on earth
Give special thanks to your nurse
As this is an article you own first

TORCH

They call me torch
Because I bring light from its source
You will not know my importance George
Unless there is darkness at its worse

With full blown darkness at the aisle
I'm effective in bringing smile
To lips of some eagles
And disappointment to bats and owls

As darkness brings delight
To those who love it at night
I also bring the same right
To those who love day light

AN AXE

Shame on you humans!
Why do you make me in tons?
And cause me to clear forest lands
These are creatures compare to none
That do not sense, talk or run

Just because to feed your greed
This does not get extinguish indeed
Even if you have the whole forest cleared
And have me labor freed
Until I become finished and buried

That is why when you mishandle me
I cut and inflict terrible pain on your knee
To revenge my fellow creatures made to be
The bushes, forests and trees
I wish they hear and see

HOE

You human, I wonder if without me you can survive
Before cultivation, you use me to clear a farm to get alive
During cultivation, you clash me with a mud and soil type
To the extent of losing some weight as if cut with a knife

When you lose one of your fellows
You call me to summon my fellow hoes
To dig the grave and bury them with bows
When work is over, you imprison us in rows
Waiting for another hard labor to blow

All these I do without feeding and payment
Even a slave is given food at the end
Yet you cry for justice brand
You cannot expect one if to me you can't budge

HOSPITAL

They call me hospital sanctuary
I play host to those giving birth to allay worry
And those who are sick to come out merry
I also send to grave gallery
Those who did not accept my hospitality

In that capacity I'm a transit camp post
Through which all human pass
From creation to life nest
And from life back to creator trust
There is no other option to chase

I'm also a bridge on earth
And like any bridge stretch
If I become old and break my length
There will be no more birth
And there will be no more death

A STRANGE DREAM IN DEED

One day with empty stomach I pulled myself on a bed
The hunger pangs were active posing a threat
Then they disappeared bit by bit
Opening a way for a panoramic parade
Which I now describe as you wait

I was ushered in a room for dining
Where array of grilled fishes were in waiting
Because I was hungry the bigger one was worth picking
It was cold and almost rotting
So under my supervision I ordered for re; warming

I turned the fish to warm the opposite side on rack
And when I turned it the second time ready for pick
It rolled itself up and stood alive intact
Then changed to a human being sitting erect
With his live eyes gazing at me direct

When I wanted to go for another treat
I woke up finding myself thirsty like a seed
To quench the burning thirst breed
I rushed for a cup of water with speed
It was a strange dream indeed!

SPEED

High speed even though for a drill
Gives a sensation of thrill
Before it kills
Leaving behind unpaid bills

Never attempt to be lured to lead
The competition with high speed
For if you attempt to be ahead
You are already dead

Follow the advice of a sage
Impregnated with popular adage
Go on a low speed mileage
If you want to arrive with age

GREATNESS THAT DISAPPEARED WITH A DREAM (I)

Tired, exhausted and broke
With only one pound in stock
His dear pocket was in shock
He sat near a tea seller on a block
Waiting for his turn as prorogued

To order a cup of black tea as he looked
And to pay the cost at stroke

While waiting in the yard
To deep sleep he was already on board
In the sleep he met warriors moving forward
To fight for a young queen in court
They were going to defend her kingdom port
Under a threat of foreign odds
He joined them on foot with his sword

Not before long in a dual
One horse men was killed signaling a downfall
But the horse ran back to their side behind the wall
He mounted the horse dashing back like a ball
And with vigor and gallantry that won her approval
The result was the dispersal
And defeat of the enemy final

GREATNESS THAT DISAPPEARED WITH A DREAM (II)

That tricked the young Queen on
And proposed a wife husband bond
A royal heroic colorful wedding was done
Inviting all dignitaries of the Queen's land
He was hailed as he shone like moon
And made in charge alone
Of royal army and treasury cone

As he wanted to spend as a duke Cock
His first night with a Queen on a hotel Rock

A tragedy came to him and knocked
He was jerked off by his horse over a log
When he was reviewing the troops in blocks
But when the horse wanted to kick him as it ran amok
He escaped with a jump of a frog

Immediately as he ran
He found himself awake and stunned
As he was being scolded by the tea owner with fun
For keeping away customers at hand
As he was occupying a wide space on land
And releasing sounds like fire gun
Unbecoming of gentleman

Realizing clearly
That he is back to poverty
And under shame and hunger mercy
He went to the other worthy
Far away tea seller of advanced parity
Ordered a cup of tea quickly
And disappeared into oblivion quietly

A DREAM THAT PAID OFF

She could not sleep
Children were hungry deep
And as the morning would creep
They were going to school to reap
No tea, no bread, no milk, no beef
To ward off the morning cold drift
Coming down the mountain cliff

DR. BELLARIO AHOY NGONG GENG

She would welcome 50 pounds gift
To meet their needs before they slipped

Those were thoughts to tow
Before sleep carried her slow
To the other side of life show
In response to her prayer vows
An honorable lady she knows
Offered her 300 dollars through a window
But she declined the offer with a bow
Arguing she also needed that amount draw
To take care of children as she was a widow

Morning broke
And was awaken by children's knock
Preparing to go to school on the rock
And asking Mom for breakfast snack
There was nothing to offer, no joke
So children went to school, no talk
With hunger pains strokes
Gnawing their bellies with hooks
She pretended to be asleep, no look

When children had gone to their destination
She dashed to the dream lady on mission salvation
Politely pleading to bring back her donation
As she realized there was a real desperation
Confused but understanding the situation
The lady gave her 600 dollars denomination
Double the amount in the dream configuration
By that it was the first and last dream formulation
In history of dreams that have paid off in action

SEARCHING THE SAGE'S MIND

With beckoning smile and a tender touch
They enter the mind of a sage
This is a house with interior wall
Decorated with a mosaic detail
The floor was laid with carpet
Similar to that of the oriental King

The sage welcomes them in a resplendent sofa
Prepared for the important guests
After setting the stage
The sage started his long exposition
Responding to the queries of his inquisitive guests

An idea is a father of planning
A good plan is a father of implementation
A good implementation is a father of good results
A good result is a father of development
Development is a father of comfortable life

Comfortable life generates new ideas
And the cycle starts again
In an upward spiral
Until one reaches
The destination and beyond

But shall we reach the end
Of human development
No that is far fetched
But we can get good life
As it is peaceful and prosperous

DR. BELLARIO AHOY NGONG GENG

HISTORY PROVIDES BRICKS

We wallow in present affairs
Grappling with dos and not to do
While nature watches at us wondering
What hell we are doing?
With our bare hands and empty minds
Without historical lessons with us
As history provides bricks
With which we build the future

We sweat putting together data
Of the recent events
Hiring experts to create and manipulate
In putting together plans for the future
Hoping that we shall achieve their goals
Without historical lessons with us
As history provides bricks
With which we build the future

Woe to those who neglect history
Thinking that they can do without
The fact is that history accounts for successes
Failures and omissions of people in the past
Those who emulate successes and avoid failures succeed
And those who do not know history will beat around the bush
As history provides bricks
With which we build the future

PLAN AND IT'S EXECUTION

Plan walks in a straight line
Never stepping on any other feet
It is also bright and shinny
Execution walks in a zigzag line
Taking a drunkard posture
It is also rough with dark complexion

Execution walks along
The failing side of a plan
Rarely does it walk following
The foot path of a plan
Or on the successful side of it
If it does, it is a miracle

Take care, Oh planners!
If you want the execution to be successful
By collecting the most detailed
Data on the subject
As both plan and execution feed on the data
As well as on the resources

www.ingramcontent.com/pod-product-compliance
Lightning Source LLC
Chambersburg PA
CBHW030250010526
44107CB00053B/1647